The GRANDPAS' Book

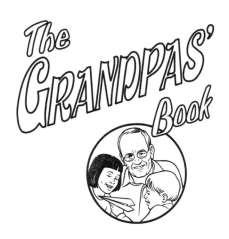

The GRANDPAS' Book

FOR THE GRANDPA WHO'S

Best AT Everything

by JOHN GRIBBLE

SCHOLASTIC INC.

New York   Toronto   London   Auckland
Sydney   Mexico City   New Delhi   Hong Kong

Library of Congress Cataloging-in-Publication data is available.

ISBN: 978-0-545-13396-8

First published in Great Britain in 2008 by
Michael O'Mara Books Limited
www.mombooks.com

Text copyright © 2008 by Michael O'Mara Books Limited
Cover image and illustrations © 2008 by David Woodroffe
Cover design by Angie Allison from an original design by www.blacksheep-uk.com

12 11 10 9 8 7 6 5 4 3 2 1   10 11 12 13 14 15/0

Printed in the U.S.A.   23
First American edition, March 2010

*To my grandson, Zack, who has brought
a new dimension to my life . . . and to "bump"
and any other grandchildren to follow!*

Contents

CONTENTS

Introduction

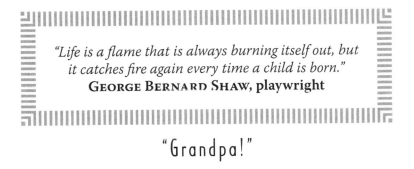

"Life is a flame that is always burning itself out, but it catches fire again every time a child is born."
GEORGE BERNARD SHAW, playwright

"Grandpa!"

You can't believe your ears. Your grandchild has learned your name — and it's the first time you've heard the word cross those tiny lips. The adorable grin and outstretched arms are irresistible. In such magic moments the special relationship between grandfather and grandchild is born.

Grandpa, you're hooked!

So begins the wonderful new phase in your life in which you begin to forge the bond of care, affection, and fun that is at the heart of being a grandfather. It is a new alliance that will endure for the rest of your life and transform the way you think and feel. This new life — so closely connected to your own — will not fail to inspire and rejuvenate you.

When your own children were growing, you were probably too busy working to enjoy the daily trials and triumphs of fatherhood as much as you would have liked — and almost certainly too exhausted by the sleepless nights and extra burden of responsibility. But now you may have the time and freedom to be alert to each new development and idiosyncrasy. Before long, you will find yourself scanning your new grandchild's face for genetic resemblances and you will feel intense pride when Grandma says, "He's got your nose, you know." As your grandchild grows, you may also spot facial expressions and body language that you recognize as your own, especially if you are lucky enough to be able to spend a lot of time together.

Of course, one of the great joys of being a grandpa is to explore the new roles you can adopt in this relationship. You can get into trouble together. You might find yourself dancing, singing, or telling stories. You may plan adventures and trips. You could manufacture toys, or devise games and imaginative worlds together. You might change your will, invest in savings bonds, and studiously investigate schools, colleges, and careers. You may become the child's confidant and guardian angel. Or you might simply have a great time reliving your own childhood.

Unwittingly, you will become a different person in the eyes of those who've known you for years, particularly Grandma and your own kids. You may find yourself becoming the object of their astonishment and amusement — and then their admiration. Before long, your grandchild will want to buy presents that you'll like or to devise a special performance for your birthday, and you'll realize the important place you have earned for yourself in your grandchild's heart.

This book, therefore, is a celebration of the unique relationship that is shared by a grandfather and a grandchild. It reveals bright ideas for having fun together. It illustrates the power of the bond that can grow between old and young. It provides practical advice to help care for your grandchild, and for his or her future. And it is an enthusiastic companion for any man who wants to fully savor the good fortune of being a grandparent.

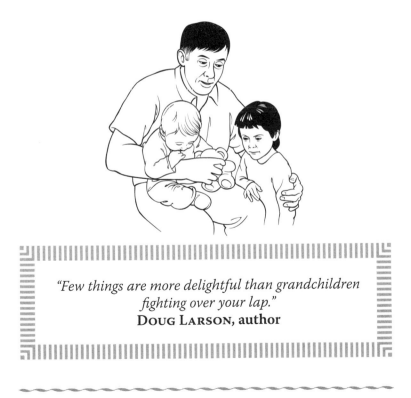

"Few things are more delightful than grandchildren fighting over your lap."
DOUG LARSON, author

So — You're a Grandpa!

Becoming a grandpa is a life-changing moment. You will find yourself exhibiting some unusual behaviors, such as tearing up the first time you see the newborn baby that is your grandchild. As time goes by, other unexpected behaviors will emerge, and before you know it you'll be a full-fledged grandfather, speaking in silly voices and showing off your corny magic tricks with the best of them.

Some signs that you are becoming a true grandpa:

* You buy a round of drinks for everyone
for the first time in living memory.

* You have "Hickory Dickory Dock" on permanent repeat
in your head when you're trying to get to sleep.

* You start talking about twenty years ahead
instead of forty years ago.

✳ You spend more time in the local toy store
than at the garden center.

✳ The TV remote defaults to kids' cartoons
rather than the movie channel.

✳ You find yourself scanning the newspapers for articles
about the current state of education rather than the current
state of your favorite sports team.

✳ At breakfast, you absentmindedly cut the crusts off your
toast — and then save the remnants for the ducks.

✳ The seat of your pants gets dirty from your ride on the
seesaw rather than from sitting on the park bench.

✳ You take more photographs than you ever
thought possible.

✳ People notice the wrinkles around your grin rather
than those around your chin — you've become "Gramps"
instead of "Grumps."

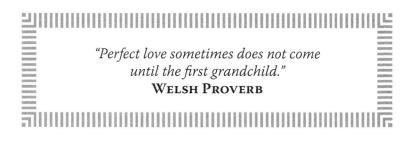

*"Perfect love sometimes does not come
until the first grandchild."*
WELSH PROVERB

Refresher Course

However hip and "with it" you think you are, you'll find that times have changed since you were last faced with the task of changing a diaper. Modern child-care methods and theories seem to differ with every passing week, so what worked perfectly well for you when you were raising your kids might now be greeted with exclamations of horror. It's important, therefore, to try to keep up with the changing times so that you are seen as being capable of taking care of a precious new baby.

Some things to watch out for that may have changed since you raised your own children:

✳ The standard advice these days when putting babies down to sleep safely is to lay them on their backs in the "feet to foot" position, in other words with their feet at the bottom of the crib. Make sure the room is well ventilated, and do not put blankets or pillows in the crib. This is very different from the old days, when parents were told to put their children facedown in a warm room, covered in thick blankets — in fact, it's a wonder anyone survived into the next generation.

✳ Nowadays parents are advised to wait until their babies are six months old before starting them on solid food, so the average weaning age is much later. Beware, too, that many parents are very particular now about what sort of food will pass their child's precious lips. For some, only organic, homemade, healthful meals will do! So although it might amuse you to see your grandchild's sucked-lemon expression when you give him or her a little sip of your beer, you may

find the parents are not so entertained. Similarly, it's probably not a good idea to produce huge handfuls of candy for the little ones every time you see them (at least not while Mom is in the room).

✳ Safety is more of an issue these days, and rules and regulations regarding the use of equipment such as car seats are much tighter, so make sure you're up to date. You may have many happy memories of wielding a hammer at the age of three while helping your own grandfather with some carpentry, but it would be wise to check with the parents before attempting such experiments yourself. You will probably also have enjoyed far greater freedom in your own youth in comparison to today's new generation, who sadly spend more time in cars being ferried from one activity to another than climbing trees and splashing around in muddy puddles. Encourage the parents to relax by all means, but be aware that the world has changed and respect the parents' boundaries.

✳ The amount of "stuff" the average baby has these days has probably quadrupled since your day. No doubt you were happy to play with a stick and a ratty cardboard box when you were a child. However, it is usual for children these days to have more possessions than the sultan of Brunei, so try to bite your tongue when the parents moan about how they can barely afford the latest top-of-the-line stroller complete with alloy wheels, go-faster stripes, and an outboard motor. (Of course, as a doting grandpa you can still spoil your grandchild as much as you wish!)

* Not all changes are bad. Kids' parties these days are far more lavish affairs than the basic pizza-and-ice-cream efforts you will remember from your own child-rearing days. This can be a headache (and a major financial drain) for the parents, of course, but it does leave you free to indulge your wildest court jester fantasies. Care to dress up as a pirate to surprise your grandchild? Go for it!

How to Recognize a Grandpa

THE FOUR AGES

You believe in Santa Claus.
You don't believe in Santa Claus.
You are Santa Claus.
You look like Santa Claus.

Grandpas come in all shapes and sizes, but one thing remains constant — grandpas are "characters." They wear funny clothes such as colorful sweaters, odd hats, and old scarves. They are always playing practical jokes on the family — and in particular, teasing Grandma. They are also famous for saying the wrong thing at the wrong time to the wrong person! And they love making silly faces and rude noises, coming out with groan-worthy puns, and generally acting like big kids.

Grandpa's Words of Wisdom

Another characteristic shared by many grandfathers is a (frequently misguided) notion that the immediate family would benefit from their great wisdom. After all, with age comes experience, and grandpas are the founts of a wealth of hard-earned knowledge. The only trouble is getting anyone to listen!

What Grandpa has learned about success

* At age 4, success is not peeing in your pants.

* At age 12, success is having friends.

* At age 17, success is having a driver's license.

* At age 35, success is having money.

* At age 50, success is having money.

* At age 70, success is having a driver's license.

* At age 75, success is having friends.

* At age 80, success is not peeing in your pants.

What Grandpa has learned about growing old

* Growing old is mandatory; growing up is optional.

* Forget the health food. As you get older, you need all the preservatives you can get.

* When you fall down, you wonder what else you can do while you're down there.

* You know you're getting old when you get the same sensation from a rocking chair that you once got from a roller coaster.

* It's frustrating when you know all the answers but nobody bothers to ask you the questions.

* Time may be a great healer, but it's a lousy beautician.

* Wisdom comes with age, but sometimes age comes alone.

Grandpa's advice to children

* When your mom is mad at your dad, don't let her brush your hair.

* If your sister hits you, don't hit her back. They always catch the second person.

* You can't trust dogs to watch your food.

* Try as you might, you won't be able to hide a piece of broccoli in a glass of milk.

* The best place to be when you're sad is Grandpa's lap.

Reading and Rhyming with Grandpa

The best gift a grandfather can give his grandchild is a love of reading. Help to foster this habit with regular trips to the library and with books for birthday presents instead of the usual plastic toys. Nursery rhymes and action poems all contribute to a child's understanding and enjoyment of language, encouraging memory and clear expression in a fun and natural way. Busy parents don't always have time to spend making up rhymes and stories, which is where you come in. You will probably remember some traditional nursery rhymes from your childhood, and you might even be able to give firsthand explanations of the meanings of some of the more old-fashioned expressions. It is this handing down of knowledge and shared references through the generations that makes being a grandfather so much fun.

Grandpa the Storyteller

Even the youngest children enjoy being read to, especially if the book has clear, colorful pictures. For little ones, look for simple stories with illustrations that refer to real-life situations that the child will understand. Books of rhymes that you can read while you bounce your grandchild up and down on your knee are always a hit. Repetition is the key here, and your grandchild will not hesitate to ask you for a favorite rhyme or story to be repeated ad nauseam. Bear it as long as you can, and just remember that when they become unenthusiastic, monosyllabic teenagers you will look back fondly at this stage.

As your grandchild gets older, you can start brushing off your storytelling skills by reciting some classic fairy tales. Get a book from the library to help you remember them, though once you've reminded yourself of the tales, kids love it if you ad-lib and tell the story in your own words. Once they're familiar with the basic stories, you can start adding your own embellishments. Who says the three little pigs didn't build their houses out of jelly, plastic spoons, and spare parts from spaceships? It doesn't matter how silly you are — the point is to get them giggling. It's even better if you can work your grandchild into the story. For example, "Goldilocks and the Three Bears" is much more fun when it's your granddaughter who is playing the starring role and tasting the porridge!

Children may also enjoy listening to stories and memories from your own childhood; just be prepared to feel ancient

when you have to keep stopping to explain such antiquities as records or rotary telephones. Bringing out old photos can also enhance this pleasure. Just don't be offended if their attention span for your reminiscences is fairly short. Remember that as far as they're concerned, you're older than God, so your past is as unreal to them as the Ice Age.

If you're lucky enough to live near your grandchildren and get roped into babysitting, offer to arrive a little early and participate in the child's bedtime story. It's a magical time of day in which grandpas can form a special bond with their grandchildren. After dinner and a bath, the children will enjoy calming down and preparing for sleep with a relaxing story that stretches their imaginations. It's even better if the story leads to conspiratorial conversation and planning new adventures with Grandpa for the next day.

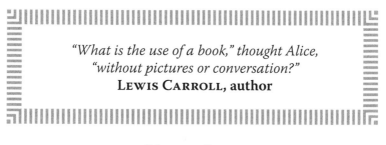

"What is the use of a book," thought Alice,
"without pictures or conversation?"
LEWIS CARROLL, author

Rhyme Time

Singing together is another great way of encouraging a child's love of language and sense of rhythm (see page 29), but if you don't trust your singing voice (or your family has banned you from singing in public), you can still recite nursery rhymes and perform the accompanying actions. An old favorite is "The Itsy-Bitsy Spider":

The itsy-bitsy spider climbed up the waterspout.
(Thumb and fingers make climbing movement.)
Down came the rain and washed the spider out.
(Fingers indicate rain falling, then sweep down and to the side.)
Out came the sun and dried up all the rain,
(Fingers of both hands make a circle for the sun,
then move upward.)
And the itsy-bitsy spider climbed up the spout again.
(Thumb and fingers make a climbing movement.)

Or how about this one? It's practically magic for a toddler:

Here's a church,
(Interlock the fingers of both hands to make a big fist,
keeping the fingers inside.)
Here's a steeple.
(Raise both forefingers together so they form a steeple shape.)
Open the door,
(Move your thumbs apart as if the "door" is opening.)
And here are the people!
(Turn your hands upside down to reveal fingers wiggling inside.)

Later, the children can be taught to perform whole rhymes and accompanying actions themselves, but first be sure to get the camcorder ready!

> *I'm a little teapot, short and stout.*
> *Here is my handle.*
> (Place one hand on a hip to imitate a handle.)
> *Here is my spout.*
> (Position the other hand in the air to imitate a spout.)
> *When I get all steamed up, hear me shout,*
> *Tip me over and pour me out!*
> (Lean over to imitate pouring tea from the spout.)

Limericks are also eternally popular with kids, and older children can have fun making up variations themselves. See if you can come up with some featuring your grandchild's name:

> *There once was a boy named Dave,*
> *Whose teddy was snatched by a wave.*
> *But Grandpa was there*
> *And rescued the bear,*
> *And everyone said he was brave!*

If you're feeling inspired, there are plenty of anthologies of rhymes for you to explore together. Nursery rhymes are a great springboard into poetry, and as your grandchild gets older, you can introduce him or her to some of the most popular modern children's poets. Shel Silverstein, Douglas Florian, Jack Prelutzky, and Roald Dahl will provide many hours of enjoyment for you both.

Famous Fictional Grandpas

Fictional grandpas are everywhere — in literature, myths and legends, stage and screen, and even fairy tales. We grow up with these archetypes as part of our cultural inheritance, and they inform our notions of what makes a grandfather. Which one of the following fictional heroes — or villains — inspires you?

Classic Grandpas in Literature

Heidi's grandfather

First impressions are not always correct. Prospects for little orphan Heidi do not seem too bright when she is sent to live with her hermit grandfather in a remote hut in the Swiss Alps. But there is no better illustration of the special bond that can develop with a grandchild than the children's classic *Heidi*, written by Johanna Spyri (1880). It portrays the growth of a warm and understanding relationship between grandfather and grandchild as Heidi's innocent trust effects a magical transformation in the gruff old man.

Grandpa Joe

One of the most popular grandfathers in literature must surely be Grandpa Joe, Charlie Bucket's jolly grandfather from Roald Dahl's novel *Charlie and the Chocolate Factory* (1964). Charlie

Bucket is a sweet-natured boy who lives with his poverty-stricken parents and his four bedridden grandparents in an overcrowded house. Next door is the largest chocolate factory in the world, a magical and secret place owned by the eccentric Willy Wonka. In what would now be viewed as a spectacular marketing coup, Wonka sparks a nationwide frenzy by circulating five special "prize" chocolate bars. Hidden inside each is a Golden Ticket that allows the finder to enter the factory for a guided tour by the famous chocolatier himself. When Charlie finds a ticket, he is surprised and delighted that Grandpa Joe jumps out of bed with excitement and agrees to accompany Charlie on the tour. The book follows their adventures as they make their way through the enchanting factory.

Grandpa Joe also turns up in the sequel, *Charlie and the Great Glass Elevator*, in which the intrepid duo ends up flying through space in an elevator!

Little Nell's grandfather

Charles Dickens's classic novel *The Old Curiosity Shop* (1840) tells the tragic and convoluted tale of Little Nell and her unnamed grandfather, who has foolishly imperiled their fortunes by gambling away Nell's inheritance at cards. Nell helps her grandfather to escape to the countryside, where further adventures await and salvation is on its way, but it turns out to be too late for Little Nell.

The Old Curiosity Shop was hugely popular in its time, though its high Victorian taste for sentimentality and melodrama was not shared by later generations. Oscar Wilde famously observed, "One would have to have a heart of stone to read the death of Little Nell without laughing."

Biblical Grandfathers

The word *grandfather* is not used in the Bible. Yet we know there were plenty of grandpas, starting with Adam. Adam's grandson was Enos, who was born when his father, Seth, was 105 years old. Adam himself reputedly lived until he was 930! However, he wasn't the oldest — that honor goes to Noah's grandfather Methuselah, who is most famous for his great age. According to the Book of Genesis, he fathered his son Lamech at the age of 187, and it is claimed that he lived for 969 years!

Another famous grandfather was Abraham, whose grandson was Jacob. Abraham was far from the stereotype of the cuddly grandfather — there are a number of stories of him smashing up his father's idols, and he agreed to sacrifice his own son, Isaac, as a test of his faith. Luckily, at the very last minute, God intervencd and spared Isaac's life by providing a ram for sacrifice instead.

Screen Grandfathers

Grampa Simpson

Grandfather to Bart, Lisa, and Maggie, Abraham J. Simpson is known to the world as Grampa in the *Simpsons* cartoon series. A hero for octogenarians everywhere, he frequently has some of the best lines in the show. For example: "Lisa . . . I know you young 'uns think we old-timers aren't any fun, but we'll show 'em. We'll show 'em all, ah, hahaha!" (He falls asleep.)

Don Vito Corleone — "The Godfather"

The Godfather trilogy, one of Hollywood's greatest epic film series, provides a colorful insight into the intimacy of Italian-American family life, and the passionate loyalty that is demanded to reinforce blood ties. It is striking that a man such as Don Corleone (played by Marlon Brando), a feared Mafia boss capable of ruthless violence to other men, shows such sensitivity and love toward his own grandchild. In fact, Don Corleone's final scene shows him playfully chasing his young grandson, Anthony, in his tomato garden. The exertion is too much for him, though, and he dies from a heart attack.

Grandpa Munster

In the 1960s TV comedy series *The Munsters*, actor Al Lewis played the part of Grandpa in a family of monsters living in a normal American suburb. Dressed in a Dracula costume, he was mischievous, cantankerous, and given to coming up with crazy ideas in his laboratory.

Making Music

There is no greater fun for you and your grandchild than being musical together. At the earliest stage, this can simply involve listening to music with him or her. You can even do this before your grandchild is born — theories abound about the benefits of playing "womb music" to the unborn child. And there are those who claim that playing Mozart will enhance the intelligence of newborn babies. Whatever the merits of these beliefs, what *is* well established is that children have musical capabilities from a very early age, and it's a capability that endures throughout life.

Babies in the womb can hear sounds beginning at twenty weeks after conception. At three months after birth, they may be seen to sway to the rhythm of music and make "musical noises": "aaah," "eee," and "ooo" (just like Grandpa!). By six months, they start imitating sounds such as "boo" or "la." And at one year, the drumming phase begins. Finally, at eighteen months, they begin to be aware of a beat in the music and to recognize different rhythms. This is a great time for Grandpa to play "the spoons" — two teaspoons held together between the fingers and tapped on the hand, thigh, and knees.

With encouragement, young children will learn the words to simple songs and will enjoy playing along with noisy instruments such as drums, tambourines, or bells. Making music together helps children to express themselves with confidence and encourages cooperation with others.

By the time they are three to five years old, children love to move to music. You might now consider buying a keyboard or xylophone as a Christmas present. With a little patient support, simple tunes will be easily learned and played.

By the age of seven, your grandchild will perform and compose with greater confidence. This is a great time for duets. At this age, some children are eager to learn an instrument, and they will start to improvise. They will also begin to take a much greater interest in pop music, if they haven't already.

A good activity for Grandpa and grandchild at this age is the DJ game. Take turns at doing an improvised introduction to the "next disc." If you're a high-tech grandpa, you could take this to the next level by downloading songs from the Internet and burning customized CDs that you think your grandchildren will enjoy. Kids love old Motown, Beatles, and rock 'n' roll, and they will be receptive to some classical music if you choose carefully. Blow up a photo of your grandchild for the CD cover and you will have a gift he or she will treasure.

Some tips for enjoying music together:

✳ Try to listen to music that you both enjoy.

✳ Dancing together adds to the fun.

✳ Mix up the musical menu. Let them listen to pop, classical, rock, or folk.

✳ Libraries are a good source to try before you buy. Aim to find a diverse range of musical experiences for your grandchildren. Why not introduce them to brass bands, reggae, world music, and jazz?

Action Songs

It's part of Grandpa's job description to make a fool of himself, and doing silly song-and-dance routines is right up there in every good grandfather's act. Action songs are also great learning experiences, and they can provide some hilarious photos for the family album. Some simply involve you singing and clapping while your grandchild imitates your actions, but even this will benefit the child: Clapping and tapping help to develop motor skills in the hands and fingers, and enhance the child's sense of rhythm. Action songs also allow children to participate, even when they can't yet sing all the words, and are the bridge between music and dance.

Younger kids love songs that have exciting accompanying actions or special sound effects that they can join in with or anticipate, such as the "pop" in "Pop Goes the Weasel" (make a popping noise with your finger on the inside of your cheek).

As children get older, they will love to sing themselves. At the age of three, many can begin to reproduce a simple tune. As the grandpa, you can play a key part in your grandchild's discovery of music by singing with him or her at home. You don't have to be a great singer — all you need are some ideas and plenty of enthusiasm!

"Ring Around the Rosie"
To be sung holding hands in a circle.

Ring around the rosie,
A pocket full of posies,
Ashes, ashes,
We all fall down.

(Everyone falls to the floor.)

"Fishes in the Water"
Start this one down on the floor after "Ring Around the Rosie."

Fishes in the water,
Fishes in the sea,
We all jump up,
With a one, two, three!

(Jump up at the end.)

"Head, Shoulders, Knees, and Toes"

While singing this song, touch both hands to each part of the body in time with the words. Then, on the second verse, leave out the word *head*, but still do the actions. On the third verse, leave out the words *head* and *shoulders*, and so on. Finish with all the words back in, but singing as fast as possible!

Head, shoulders, knees, and toes, knees and toes.
Head, shoulders, knees, and toes, knees and toes.
And eyes and ears and mouth and nose.
Head, shoulders, knees, and toes, knees and toes!

"I Wish I Were"

This is great song for impersonators. Choose a different animal or person each time, and everyone has to sound and act like the chosen creature when singing "this way and that way."

I wish I were a kangaroo, a kangaroo, a kangaroo,
I wish I were a kangaroo, so I could play all day.
This way and that way,
This way and that way,
I wish I were a kangaroo, so I could play all day.

"This Is the Way the Lady Rides"

This is a fun action song for all kids still young enough to perch on your knee. It's sung to the tune of "Here We Go 'Round the Mulberry Bush."

This is the way the lady rides, a-trit-a-trot, a-trit-a-trot.

(Repeat once, while bouncing the child up and down calmly on your knee.)

This is the way the gentleman rides, a-gallop-a-gallop, a-gallop-a-gallop.

(Repeat, this time bouncing the child up and down vigorously on your knee.)

This is the way the farmer rides, a-hobbledee-dee, a-hobbledee-dee.

(Slowly rock the child from side to side on your knee.)

This is the way the farmer rides, a-hobbledee-dee and DOWN IN THE DITCH!

(Slowly rock, then suddenly drop the child down between your knees to within an inch of the floor.)

"Row, Row, Row Your Boat"

This is a nice, gentle lullaby, but you can add some fun, unexpected elements. For example:

Row, row, row your boat, gently to the shore,
If you see a lion, don't forget to ROAR!

(Encourage the child to join in with a mighty roar.)

Row, row, row your boat, gently to the river,
If you see a polar bear, don't forget to SHIVER!

(Encourage the child to shiver dramatically and go "Brrrrr!")

Row, row, row your boat, gently to the stream,
If you see a crocodile, don't forget to SCREAM!

(Scream "Aaaaaargh!" together.)

Most nursery rhymes can be made more fun and personal in this way, so try to think of your own endings and variations if you can.

Top tips for Grandpas

✳ Have confidence in yourself and don't worry about sounding or looking silly. Your grandchild will love you all the more for losing your inhibitions.

✳ A good time for action songs is when your grandchild is feeling lively but relaxed, maybe after a nap or a meal.

✳ An action song sometimes has the power to alter a child's mood, making him or her happier and more content.

✳ Try to get together with other grandparents or caregivers and children to play action songs as a group; the children will enjoy this social aspect of music.

✳ Action songs are a great way to make a long car trip or time spent in a line pass quickly.

Instruments

Your performance on the spoons will undoubtedly be admired and mimicked. But eventually you might want to try out some more sophisticated musical instruments. Of course, you could indulge your grandchild with a top-of-the-line grand piano, but if he or she can barely hold a sippy cup yet, there are other more economical alternatives. Here are some ideas for "instruments" for your grandchild that are fun to make and play together.

✳ **A basic banjo:** Stretch some rubber bands around an empty ice cream carton and strum away as if you're a music star!

✳ **Bottle music:** Find three or four empty glass bottles and fill each one with a different amount of water. Let your grandchild hit the rim of the bottles with a teaspoon while you supervise.

* **Plastic shakers:** Fill an empty plastic water bottle with rice, beads, or sand to make a funky shaker. Make sure you tape the lid securely so that it doesn't fly open when shaken vigorously.

* **Tin Pan Alley:** Of course, nothing beats an improvised drum set made of upside-down saucepans that can be bashed with a wooden spoon. If you're really brave, you can provide two saucepan lids for cymbals. If you're not partially deaf to start with, you will be when your grandchild has finished playing.

Let's Dance!

Dance contributes to the mental and physical development of children, and may be especially beneficial if your grandchild is very energetic and needs to burn off some energy. Most grandchildren will be able to tell Grandpa about the movement activities they do at day care or in school, and they can provide enthusiastic performances for you to appreciate. But children love it even more if the adults around them join in.

Choose a special "dance time" when your grandchild can move to music with you. Here are some ideas to get you started:

* Try "foot waltzing." Your grandchild stands on your feet and you do the dancing.

* Encourage your grandchild to move in time to a rhythm: clapping, jumping, or hopping.

* Get some play dress-up clothes and arrange a special dance performance for the parents.

In Grandpa's Footsteps?

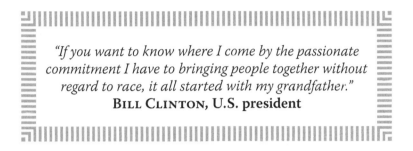

"If you want to know where I come by the passionate commitment I have to bringing people together without regard to race, it all started with my grandfather."
BILL CLINTON, U.S. president

We all have grandfathers — the rich and the poor, celebrities or civilians. Some grandfathers are famous through literature, stage, or screen; others become well known through achievement or notoriety. But what all grandpas have in common is that they can be a big influence in their grandchildren's lives — for better or worse. Here are some examples of family relationships where the younger members have followed in their grandfather's footsteps — or wandered off in a different direction altogether!

✳ Sir Winston Churchill's "hippie" granddaughter, Arabella Churchill, rebelled against her illustrious pedigree to work for a leprosy charity, and she was also one of the cofounders of the Glastonbury Festival, an open-air rock music gathering.

✳ More than sixty years after the assassination of India's spiritual leader Mahatma Gandhi, his granddaughter Ela still spreads his message of nonviolence. She demonstrated regularly for women's rights during the apartheid era in

South Africa. "Being born into this family meant campaigning, and politics were part of everyday life," she said. Despite spending several years under house arrest for her political activism, she still travels the world today, giving talks on her grandfather's philosophy.

* Alessandra Mussolini has followed in her famous fascist grandfather's footsteps by becoming a right-wing politician. She is a member of the European Parliament and was a founder and leader of the Italian neo-fascist political party Social Action.

* Sophie Dahl, the once-voluptuous British model and published children's author, has an even more famous children's author in her family — her grandfather, Roald Dahl. As a child, she was the inspiration for the character Sophie, the giant's helper, in Roald Dahl's book *The BFG*.

* Celebrated actress Dame Helen Mirren is seen as the quintessential British national treasure. She even played Elizabeth II in the recent feature film *The Queen*. Yet surprisingly, her grandfather Pyotr Vasielvich Mironov was a Russian aristocrat who went to London to buy arms, only to find himself stranded by the Bolshevik Revolution. And her great-great-great-great-grandfather was a Russian field marshal and one of the heroes of the Napoleonic wars.

Grandfatherly Dynasties

Pandit Jawaharlal Nehru — head of the great Indian political dynasty

Born in 1889, the son of a wealthy Indian barrister and politician, Nehru became one of the youngest leaders of the Indian National Congress. Alongside Mahatma Gandhi, Nehru was a charismatic, radical leader, advocating a socialist strategy to address India's needs and challenges. In 1947 he presided over Indian independence from the British empire and became the first prime minister of independent India.

Nehru's daughter, Indira Gandhi, and his grandson, Rajiv Gandhi, followed in his footsteps to become prime ministers. Both were later assassinated.

Zulfiqar Ali Bhutto — patriarch of Pakistan

Born in 1928, Bhutto was a popular Pakistani politician who served as the president of Pakistan from 1971 to 1973 and as prime minister from 1973 to 1977. He was the founder of the Pakistan Peoples Party (PPP), one of the largest and most influential political parties of Pakistan. In 1979 he was executed, following a controversial trial, on charges of conspiracy to murder a political opponent. His daughter, Benazir Bhutto, also served twice as prime minister; she was assassinated in 2007. His grandson, Bilawal Bhutto Zardari, has now become chairman of the party.

American presidential dynasties

George Herbert Walker Bush (born in 1924) was the forty-first president of the United States, serving from 1989 to 1993. His father was a senator. He was chosen by Ronald Reagan to be vice president and succeeded him in office by defeating Michael Dukakis. He is the father of George W. Bush, the forty-third president of the United States, and Jeb Bush, a former governor of Florida.

Bush is now the oldest living United States president, and he and his wife, Barbara, hold the record for the longest married presidential couple. He is grandfather to fourteen grandchildren from his five children.

Of course, one of the most famous presidential dynasties is the Kennedy clan. The family patriarch was Patrick J. Kennedy, a first-generation American of poor Irish Catholic descent. Under his influence, the family became wealthy and prominent in American politics. He was grandfather to John F. Kennedy, the thirty-fifth president of the United States; Robert Kennedy, U.S. attorney general; and Edward "Ted" Kennedy, senior United States senator from Massachusetts. Despite the family's power and glamour, they have suffered a series of tragedies sometimes called "the Kennedy curse." These include the assassinations of John F. Kennedy and Robert F. Kennedy, numerous aircraft crashes, a disastrous lobotomy, a murder conviction, and a controversial fatal car crash.

"I don't know who my grandfather was; I am much more concerned to know what his grandson will be."
ABRAHAM LINCOLN, U.S. president

Finally, a grandfather and grandson have both been presidents of the United States. William Henry Harrison took office in 1841 but died of pneumonia just thirty-one days later. Half a century later his grandson Benjamin was also elected and served from 1889 to 1893.

Michael Redgrave — actor grandfather

Michael Redgrave, star of *The Lady Vanishes*, *Mourning Becomes Electra*, and *The Dambusters*, among other classic films, was the father of Vanessa, Corin, and Lynn Redgrave, and grandfather to Natasha and Joely Richardson, Jemma and Luke Redgrave, and Carlo Nero — all actors or involved in filmmaking. Michael Redgrave was himself the son of another pair of thespians — the silent film star Roy Redgrave and the actress Margaret Scudamore.

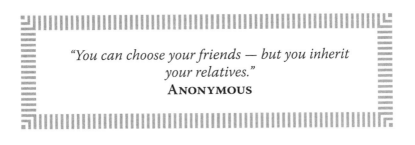

"You can choose your friends — but you inherit your relatives."
ANONYMOUS

A Grand Day Out

As a doting grandfather, you will naturally want to spend time with your grandchild as he or she is growing up. It's easy to fall into the habit of simply enjoying a regular Sunday lunch date with the extended family, but if you make the effort to get out of the house and go on occasional special outings with your grandchild, you will have a shared experience and some wonderful memories to treasure. Plus the parents will be extremely grateful to have a little time off (even more so if you return the child worn out and ready for bed). Why not suggest one of the following outings the next time you see your grandchild?

✳ Take a trip by train or bus to a nearby town to explore. The trip itself will be exciting for small children, especially if you stock up on snacks to produce at regular intervals. When you get to the destination, find a postcard of the local area and get your grandchild to write something and send it home, even if you'll be back again in a few hours! He or she will enjoy surprising his or her parents with it when it turns up in the mail the next day or so.

* Dress up in your team's colors and head to the stadium for a football or baseball game.

* Plan a picnic at the local park — and take a kite along. This is even more fun if you involve your grandchild in choosing and preparing the food beforehand.

* Kids love speeding around on wheels, and there's no reason for you not to try it again, too. Have a race with your grandchild on roller skates, scooters, bikes, or even a skateboard!

* Arrange a visit to the movies — keep an eye out for kid-friendly matinees and film clubs. Of course no trip to the movies is complete without a ridiculously oversized box of popcorn to share!

* Go to the local swimming pool for a dip together. Or find a water park with slides and chutes and give yourself a few more white hairs.

✳ Make up a series of "I spy" books according to the interests of your grandchild. For example, make a book of cars, varieties of birds or farm animals, or types of wildflowers. For children who can't read yet, you could use pictures cut from magazines. Then set off on an expedition to find as many as possible and mark them in your book.

✳ Visit the ice cream shop for a treat and allow your grandchild free rein in making up the most outrageous combination of flavors. Then stand back and marvel at how this normally fussy eater can pack away two thousand calories in ten minutes flat.

✳ Get a camera and set out to "capture" your grandchild's favorite spots in the surrounding area, then make a photo album together.

✳ Reclaim your lost youth and head for the local playground.

"Elephants and grandchildren never forget."
ANDY ROONEY, TV commentator

Grandpa's Garden

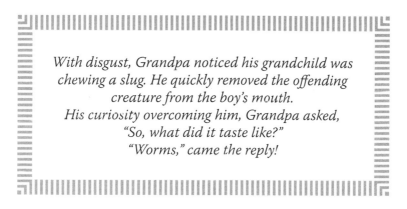

*With disgust, Grandpa noticed his grandchild was
chewing a slug. He quickly removed the offending
creature from the boy's mouth.
His curiosity overcoming him, Grandpa asked,
"So, what did it taste like?"
"Worms," came the reply!*

Most grandpas enjoy spending time in the garden, and it can
be a great delight to discover that the garden also offers plenty
of opportunities for activities to share with a grandchild. Kids
lead such busy, active lives these days that it can be valuable for
them to experience the sense of calm and contemplation that
working in a garden can bring. However, the reluctant gardener might need more of an enticement to be drawn into the
backyard. Try one of the following ideas for special projects
that will inspire little budding gardeners!

How to Build a Birdhouse

Making a gourd birdhouse

A gourd is a member of the squash family and has a shell
that becomes hard when it has dried out. Gourds come in a

number of different shapes and sizes, but you'll need to find a bottle-shaped one, ideally 8 to 12 inches in length. You can buy them or grow them yourself from seeds. (There is a variety known as a Mexican bottle gourd that is sometimes specifically sold as the "birdhouse gourd.") Gourds can make good homes for many kinds of birds, including swallows, wrens, bluebirds, and woodpeckers.

Hang the gourd in a warm, dry place until it is hard. Drill an entrance hole for the birds, approximately 1 to 1½ inches across. (The size will determine which species will be able to use the house.) Drill some additional holes in the bottom for drainage. Then get your grandchild to help you remove the seeds inside with a spoon. Once the gourd is clean, he or she can decorate it imaginatively with paint before covering it with clear varnish. Finally, suspend the house with wire in a sheltered place in the garden, at least 6½ feet from the ground.

Making a birdhouse from a carton

Clean out and completely dry a large cardboard juice carton. Seal the top securely.

Carefully cut an entrance hole for the birds on one of the sides of the carton — about 1 to 1½ inches in diameter, and 2 inches up from the bottom. Make a slit below the entrance and attach a Popsicle stick or length of dowel so that it creates a perch. Your grandchild can then help you pierce some drainage holes in the

bottom of the carton with a pencil, and paint the birdhouse and cover it with a couple of coats of clear varnish to finish. You can suspend the birdhouse over a branch or eave using a piece of wire threaded through the top.

Attracting Birds to Your Garden

So the house is built — but what can you do to invite the bird population to move in?

✻ You can lure birds to the new birdhouse by supplying water and food nearby: Try seeds, unsalted peanuts, oats, or bread crumbs.

✻ Use an old saucer to make a birdbath. Mount it on a flat board screwed to the top of a pole, then hammer the pole into the ground.

✻ It's a good idea to hang several "feeders" around the garden, as well as near the birdhouse. The greater number of different types of food you can provide, the greater variety of birds you will attract.

✻ Plant native varieties of shrubs and flowers wherever you can and try to reduce the amount of chemicals you use in your gardening. Fruits and berries are always a good source of food for birds.

✻ If you have space, a small pond will appeal to birds, and it will also attract many other forms of interesting wildlife.

All you need now is a hidden viewing spot and a pair of binoculars.

GRANDPA'S INTERESTING BIRD FACTS!

✳ An owl's bones are hollow.
✳ A hummingbird flaps its wings more than fifty times per second.
✳ The domestic chicken is probably the world's most common bird. In fact, there are more chickens in the world than people.
✳ The largest bird egg is the ostrich's. If you want to have one for your breakfast, it will take forty minutes to hard-boil!
✳ A pair of nesting barn owls are capable of catching and eating nearly three thousand rats a year.

Birding

A trip to your local bookstore or library will equip you with a birding book. This will provide pictures and information about plumage, flight patterns, and bird habitats, and it will help you identify the different varieties. It will also tell you when migratory birds might be expected to arrive or depart. You can then buy or make a birding journal to record the sightings that you make together.

With binoculars, you will be able to note and record the habits of the birds. Collecting bird feathers is another fascinating activity. It won't be long before you'll be taking a trip to a local bird sanctuary together to widen the repertoire of your bird sightings.

Get Digging

Taking your grandchild on a walk around the garden to appreciate the colors and aromas of plants is a special experience. The following activities are great ways to encourage an early interest in gardening, as they are both easy and rewarding.

Potted plants

Using flowerpots and containers for flowering plants is fun for children because they can label them with the plant's name or even decorate the pots to provide a splash of color while waiting for the flower to grow. Try planting crocus and daffodil bulbs in the autumn (but keep in mind that both bulbs are poisonous if ingested). Leave them on a sunny window ledge, water them regularly, and they will be a magical discovery for the child when the flowers raise their heads in early spring.

Sunflower seeds

Kids always seem fascinated by sunflowers. It must be a combination of the jolly name and the fact that they are so easy to grow. Plant the seeds just after the last frost of the year in a sunny spot in the garden. You can also buy some varieties that can be grown in large pots. For the giant sunflowers, it's best to plant them near a fence so you can tie them back to protect them against the wind. The seedlings should start to pop out of the ground within two weeks. They will start slowly, but they'll pick up speed quickly. Why not organize a competition to see who can grow the tallest plant?

The vegetable patch

Vegetables are a good choice for kids to grow since they germinate quickly and you have the added benefit of being able to eat them once they've grown! You can make suggestions for which vegetables to plant (squash, carrots, and pumpkins are all good choices), but it's more fun to let your grandchildren choose for themselves after looking through the seed packets and catalogs.

You can buy special-size garden tools so that grandchildren can participate fully in digging, planting, marking the seed rows with sticks, watering, and weeding. You might consider allocating a separate area for the vegetables so that the children really feel ownership of the seedlings, but be prepared for them to stomp around the rest of the garden getting muddy and "weeding" your most prized flowers — it's all part of the fun!

Make sure you take photographs of your gardening activities so you have a record of your garden growing. And consider placing a little bench near the vegetable patch. Maybe your bench will even have a good view of the birdhouse!

How to Make a Scarecrow

Every gardener loves birds — until the birds gobble up your precious plants. So why not make a scarecrow to protect your seedlings? It's both fun and practical.

Start with the head. Stuff an old pillowcase or sewn-together sheet with hay, which you can buy at a pet store. Sew on buttons for eyes and use colorful material to make the nose, mouth, and ears. Add one of Grandma's old hats for a finishing touch.

For the body, stuff an old shirt and pants with hay. Sew the parts together with garden twine and thread a long stick through the arms of the shirt so that your scarecrow can be suspended. It can then be dangled from a tree branch so that it swings in the wind. Or prop the scarecrow up on an old chair or bench. You can even try different poses for fun!

Bug Hunting with Grandpa

Insects can be big pests for the gardener, but they are also fascinating to observe. Try organizing a bug hunt with your grandchild. Even the most urban backyards can be home to caterpillars, moths, butterflies, and ladybugs. Equip your grandchild with a jar and a magnifying glass and let the hunt begin.

The bugs should be carefully collected in the jar for later scrutiny and identification. You may even want to create a booklet for Mom or Dad with drawings, photographs, and notes describing what you have found. Remember to return the bugs afterward to the place where they were found to encourage a respect for all living things.

Making a Wormery

A wormery is simply a temporary home for earthworms so that you can study their movements. Most children find this activity completely fascinating!

For a basic wormery, you can simply use an empty, clean two-liter plastic bottle with the top cut off. Drill a few small holes in the bottom for drainage.

To make the wormery habitable for its occupants, add a layer of moistened shredded newspaper at the bottom. Then add a layer of sand and another of soil. (You'll be able to see how the worms move and mix the layers.) The next layer should be a mixture of materials such as manure, leaf litter, or compost, then add some more soil and strips of moistened newspaper to finish.

Now, find some earthworms and pop them into their new home (naming them is optional)! Finally, add a scattering of food such as kitchen vegetable scraps or eggshells on top. Don't add too much food, though, as you don't want to overfeed the worms.

Leave the wormery in a cool, dark location for a few weeks. Keep it covered with cardboard or card stock to retain moisture and keep out flies. Make sure it is well ventilated — it shouldn't be too hot or too wet. Your grandchild will delight in telling his or her friends about Grandpa's special worm collection.

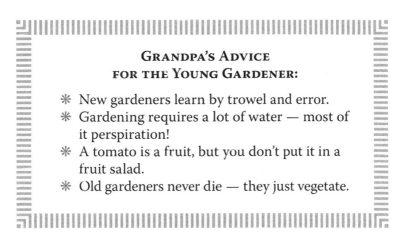

GRANDPA'S ADVICE
FOR THE YOUNG GARDENER:

* New gardeners learn by trowel and error.
* Gardening requires a lot of water — most of it perspiration!
* A tomato is a fruit, but you don't put it in a fruit salad.
* Old gardeners never die — they just vegetate.

Nocturnal Goings-on

Most wildlife visits the garden at night. Why not challenge your grandchildren to detect evidence of nocturnal animals in your garden? Help them look for footprints (tracks), burrows, pathways, chewing marks, feathers, and droppings.

Can I Have a Pet, Grandpa?

"Can I have a pet, pleeeease?"

Those words strike fear into the heart of any self-respecting parent. But every once in a while, a child will catch his parents in a good mood and they will agree to this request. Which is where you come in. Deciding which pet to choose is a great responsibility, and a man of your wisdom and experience is just the person to consult.

Incidentally, it should go without saying that the fast track to ending up in the doghouse yourself is to get a pet for the child without first consulting Mom and Dad!

It should also go without saying that you adopt a pet for life, not just for Christmas, however appealing it looks in the store or shelter. That cute little puppy will one day grow into a great big slobbering dog, which might not be so suitable for a small apartment in a high-rise building. So choose with care.

A Dog, Perhaps?

Dogs are probably the favorite choice for most children. After all, they are loyal, playful, obedient, and absolutely adorable when they're puppies. Dogs are truly man's best friend.

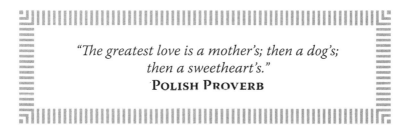

"The greatest love is a mother's; then a dog's; then a sweetheart's."
POLISH PROVERB

But which breed to choose?

The dog should be selected according to the size of the house, the age (and size!) of the grandchild, the pet maintenance budget, the ability of the owners to take it out on walks, and the temperament and needs of the breed itself. Each breed brings its own "image" and risks.

Bear in mind that there's a cost to owning and caring for a pet, both in terms of financial outlay and time. The dog will need to be walked, it will need to eat, it will need the vet, it will need to be trained, and it may need to be insured. Your enthusiasm for getting a dog for your grandchild may wilt slightly if it becomes apparent that you are expected to take care of some of this.

"A door is what a dog is perpetually on the wrong side of."
OGDEN NASH, humorist

Maybe a Cat, Then?

Cats are also a good choice to consider for a pet. They are well known for their sense of curiosity and their independent nature, and they are eager to explore everything — from an empty paper bag to the compost heap and the microwave oven! Some cats are affectionate and cuddly, but others are aloof, do not like to be petted, and will use their claws to reach the ceiling by climbing the curtains. If possible, try to spend a bit of time with the kitten before agreeing to take it home so you can find out which type of personality it has.

Cats like freedom, but an outdoor cat is at risk of injuries from fighting, disease, poisoning, and traffic accidents. Outdoor cats are a nuisance to neighbors and can often be found digging in gardens and marking their territory. They can also kill songbirds and other wildlife. So if you do decide to keep your kitten indoors, you will need to train it to use a litter box. It's very easy: Simply provide your kitten with a clean box half full of cat litter in a convenient, quiet location, and take it there on a regular basis following meals and naps until it gets the idea.

How About a Rabbit?

Rabbits are friendly, intelligent, cuddly, and very appealing at first sight. They can live happily indoors or outdoors. However, their hutch needs to be cleaned regularly, and they can occasionally scratch or bite, so for this reason they are not considered suitable pets for small children. Rabbits are happier if they have a partner, so two rabbits are better than one.

Grandpa will, of course, be expected to construct a sound wooden hutch. A hutch should be at least 60 x 23 x 23 inches.

Tips for keeping your rabbit healthy

* Give it your time and attention — it should be checked at least twice a day.

* Feed it at least once a day and insure it has a good, balanced diet, including hay, dark leafy green vegetables,

good-quality pellets, and fruits such as apples (without the seeds).

✳ Change and provide fresh water at least once a day.

✳ Clean its water bottle and food bowls daily.

✳ Its housing should be dry and cleaned once a week with a mild nontoxic disinfectant. Never use bleach or household cleansers.

✳ Ensure there are no extreme or sudden changes in temperature.

✳ Let it play and exercise daily.

✳ Provide a litter box and clean it every day.

✳ Rabbits' teeth grow continuously, so give a rabbit gnawing blocks and chew toys to help wear them down.

✳ Long-haired rabbits need daily grooming; short-haired rabbits need weekly grooming.

If all this sounds like too much work, perhaps the best pet to consider is a toy puppy or kitten!

Grandpa's Party

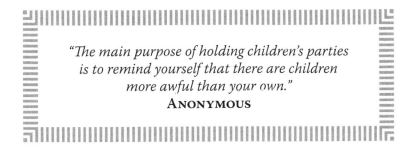

"The main purpose of holding children's parties is to remind yourself that there are children more awful than your own."
ANONYMOUS

All children look forward to their birthday parties with great excitement, but moms and dads are so busy these days, especially if they both have jobs, that it can be difficult for them to come up with enough ideas to make the occasion memorable. This is where you can help, and dazzle your grandchild and his or her friends in the process.

Setting the Scene

Preparing the invitations is a fantastic challenge and a great opportunity for you and your grandchild to work on a project together. Choosing a theme for the party is the first order of business, so let your imaginations run free. For example, your theme might be pirates, "in the pink," pop stars, a beach party, a jungle safari, princesses, a teddy bears' picnic, or a pool party.

Once the theme is chosen, the design of the invitations can be done imaginatively on a computer by using clip art or downloaded images, or by letting your grandchild get out his or her crayons and glue and make them him- or herself. The invitation will need to provide all the basic practical details about the date, place, and time of the party, but it can also specify attire (party dresses or sneakers), some of the party activities (karaoke or fashion show), and whether guests should bring or prepare anything (an eye patch or a pink hat).

Next, you'll need to decorate.

Grandpas of modest ambition will tie a few balloons to the mailbox with a sign saying JOHNNY IS 7 TODAY or PARTY HERE! But the more enterprising grandfather will produce giant cardboard pirates to stand on the front lawn or wrap his car in pink tissue paper so that guests say, "Wow — *there's* the party!" as they drive up the street.

Planning the Food

The art of good leadership and quality party preparation is asking for help. It's likely that you and your grandchild will quickly reach the conclusion that you will need assistance with the party food. It is important to plan a list of the basic cuisine desired. The standard cupcakes and lemonade need no explanation, but the more elaborate and unusual requests (a pirate ship birthday cake with twenty-four cannons?) should be planned far in advance.

If Grandma or another adult friend or relative is a master baker, try to enlist this person's assistance. Or buy an elaborate cake at your local bakery or supermarket.

Personnel

Everyone who has ever run a children's party knows that you can never have too many supervisors. A creative grandpa can provide some extra staff for the party by contacting the local Boy or Girl Scout groups to see if some older (responsible!) children would like to help.

Grandpa's Role

Having guaranteed that supervision is assigned to lots of people other than yourself, you will be free to be the life and soul of the party.

This is where both duplicity and duplication come to the fore.

You can invent Great-uncle Fred and introduce him as your twin brother. Great-uncle Fred is the exact replica of you (in fact, he *is* you), but he wears a different sweater, glasses, and perhaps a false mustache or a wig.

This clever device gives you a great deal of flexibility in your management of the party. Whenever one of the children asks a rude question or behaves inappropriately, you can "just go and fetch Great-uncle Fred" to see what he thinks about the issue. The ruse allows you the chance for a rest when needed. You can also maintain your reputation for being "nice," while poor Great-uncle Fred takes the rap for being the disciplinarian.

Party Games for Younger Kids

First, you will need to equip yourself with prizes for the party games.

The following games should all ensure a party to remember, especially if they're given the special Grandpa twist.

Please, Mr. Porter, Can We Cross the Water?

TRADITIONAL VERSION

An adult takes on the role of "Mr. Porter" and stands in the middle of an area designated by two lengths of rope on the floor. The children are lined up along one rope facing him.

The children all shout, "Please, Mr. Porter, can we cross the water?"

Mr. Porter selects a color or an item of clothing and says, "Only if you are wearing jeans" or "Only if you are wearing something red." Only those children may cross the water safely. Those remaining must run away, and Mr. Porter chases them. The first one caught then becomes the new Mr. Porter.

Play the game in the backyard and instead of tagging them with your hand, use a water-squirter!

Pass the Package

TRADITIONAL VERSION

Wrap a present such as a bar of chocolate in a number of layers of paper. The package is passed around the circle of children while music plays. When the music is stopped, the child holding the package unwraps one layer and the music resumes. When the music stops again, the child with the package unwraps another layer. The winner is the child who unwraps the final layer and reveals the prize.

GRANDPA'S ALTERNATIVE VERSION

Play the game, but with dares. Write an instruction on the inside of each layer of paper, so the child left holding the package in each round must also do a dare. These could include things like sing a song, eat a bowl of mushy peas, swap shoes with someone else, and so on (your grandchild will no doubt happily come up with a few ideas).

Line-up competitions

TRADITIONAL VERSION

In these games, the children at the party line up into teams. Each team has to transfer some object along the line. The team to complete the race first wins the game.

GRANDPA'S ALTERNATIVE VERSIONS

* An orange held under the chin has to be passed along the line from neck to neck.

* A balloon is gripped between the knees of the first member of the team, who then has to circle the line of the team before passing the balloon to the next team member — from knees to knees.

The Human Knot

TRADITIONAL VERSION

All the children stand in a circle. Each child must use his or her right hand to take hold of the left hand of another child anywhere in the circle (but not the child on either side of him or her). Then each child must use his or her left hand to take hold of the right hand of another child in the circle.

The whole group then has to work together to unwind the knot. The result should be a perfect circle!

GRANDPA'S ALTERNATIVE VERSION

Play the traditional version, but divide the group into two teams and make it a race.

Obstacle races

TRADITIONAL VERSION

It is good to play this game in the backyard or in a large room. Start by setting out two lines of obstacles. Examples could be sacks (to be jumped into and "hopped"), blankets (to be wriggled under), jump ropes (to be used for a set number of jumps), hula hoops (to be swung around the stomach a number of times), a set of clothes (to be put on, then taken off), etc. Two teams then compete to finish the obstacle race in the fastest time.

GRANDPA'S ALTERNATIVE VERSIONS

* Do the race with each person wearing a blindfold.

* Include some "horrible" things to eat (like anchovies) as one of the obstacles.

* Make everyone run backward!

Musical Chairs

TRADITIONAL VERSION

Position some chairs in a circle. There should be one fewer than the number of children at the party. The children dance around the chairs until the music stops, and then rush to sit in one of the seats. The player who fails to find a seat is eliminated. Remove one of the chairs each time so that ultimately there is only one winner sitting in the "last remaining seat."

GRANDPA'S ALTERNATIVE VERSION

Before the players sit down, they must complete a task that Grandpa gives out before each round. Tasks can include spinning in a circle, doing five jumping jacks, or bending down to touch one's toes.

Musical Statues

TRADITIONAL VERSION

The children dance around the room to music. When the music stops, each child must "freeze" like a statue and not move, speak, or even change facial expression. Anyone who moves is "out," and play continues until only one child is left. (If you're judging, try to make the children laugh by making faces at them!)

GRANDPA'S ALTERNATIVE VERSION

An alternative that requires no music is Dead Fishes. In this version, the children parade around the room until "Dead fishes!" is shouted. They then have to fall on the floor immediately and not move a muscle until you say so.

Games for Older Kids

Chinese Whispers

Divide the group into two teams. Team 1 leaves the room while Team 2 chooses a pantomime to act out, such as changing a baby's diaper or mounting a camel.

One member of Team 1 is brought back into the room and told the mime. A second member of Team 1 is brought into the room to watch the mime performed by the first team member. A third member is brought back to watch the performance by team member 2, and so on. The final member of Team 1 has to state what he or she thinks the mime shows.

Egyptian Mummies

Split the group into teams and give each a full roll of toilet paper. Each team wraps a volunteer in the toilet paper so that he or she looks like an Egyptian mummy. The first team to finish the roll is the winner!

Quack, Ducky, Quack

Someone is selected to be blindfolded and is handed a pillow. Everyone else sits on chairs in a circle, swapping places so that the blindfolded person doesn't know who is sitting where. The blindfolded child then places the pillow on the lap of one of those seated and says, "Quack, ducky, quack." The owner of the lap must quack. The object of the game is for the blindfolded person to try to guess the identity of the "quacker."

Dance Fever

In order to really excite the children before the party ends, dancing is essential. If you're indoors, it's probably a good idea to push some furniture out of the way to create a dance floor. Try the following song for a memorable end to a great party.

"The Hokey Pokey"

For this song the children must stand in a circle and join in with the actions, waving their arms, legs, etc., into the middle and then outside the circle. The "hokey pokey" action involves wiggling while turning in a circle.

You put your right arm in,
You put your right arm out,
You put your right arm in,
And you shake it all about,
You do the Hokey Pokey,
And you turn yourself around,
That's what it's all about!

[Second verse]

You put your left arm in,
You put your left arm out [etc.]

[Third verse]

You put your right leg in,
You put your right leg out [etc.]

[Fourth verse]

You put your left leg in,
You put your left leg out [etc.]

[Fifth verse]

You put your whole self in,
You put your whole self out [etc.]

Grandpa the Babysitter

Babysitting! So *that's* why grandparents were created. In case you're ever called upon to babysit without the added assistance of Grandma, it's best to be prepared for the challenges of the job.

*"The writing on the wall means
the grandchildren found the crayons."*
ANONYMOUS

Unfortunately, grandpas seem to be genetically programmed to wind up kids to a point of overexcitement before they happily hand them back to Mom at the end of the day. However, if you're babysitting, you will find you actually need to calm the children down to get them to go to sleep. This can be a rude awakening for some grandpas.

Babysitting requires multitasking. For example, you might have to change a dirty diaper while making sure the bathwater isn't too hot and while keeping the baby from eating too much toilet paper.

Grandpas are generally not designed for multitasking.

In addition, babies are born with an intuitive understanding that their normal behavior must completely change whenever Grandpa is the babysitter.

Baby Jekyll normally looks happily at his or her picture book, sucks contently at a bottle, and coos appreciatively as he or she is lowered into the crib for an uninterrupted night's sleep.

Baby Hyde takes pleasure in ripping out the first three pages of the book and puking the milk all over Grandpa's favorite sweater, all the while revealing that his or her vocal cords can match the whine of an air-raid siren. Baby Hyde seldom allows him- or herself to be lowered into the crib — let alone considers sleep when he or she gets there. And in the unlikely event that Baby Hyde does drift off, it's highly likely that Mom will call at exactly that point to make sure baby is all right!

The only way to survive all of this is to be prepared. You must take a professional approach to your duties. The following pointers should help.

DO:

* Arrive at least twenty minutes before the parents are to leave. This will give you time to run through what's expected, such as the bedtime rituals and bathing routines.

* Make sure you know which songs must be sung and whether you will be expected to dance.

* Demand a briefing from Mom and Dad about the names of the teddy bear, the dog, and the blanket and which ones need to be kissed before lights out. (Oh, and make sure you find out whether lights *do* go out or not!)

* You need to know where diapers are kept and where the smelly diapers are to be dumped.

* You'll need to be trained on the operation of the baby monitor, if there is one. Otherwise, the baby might end up listening to you all night rather than vice versa.

* If the children are older, seek guidance about which TV channels or Web sites they can visit and whether "adult" sites have been filtered (have a separate conversation with Mom and Dad about this if necessary).

* Before the parents leave, agree on a time to expect their return home. Make them swear not to be late (a signed contract is best), and stress that you will change your will if they are.

* Make sure you have Mom's and Dad's cell phone numbers. Have them turn them on before they leave. Persuade Mom to put her phone in one of her pockets rather than in her enormous handbag.

* Ask for the address and telephone number of the people or place Mom and Dad are visiting.

* Make sure you have all the relevant emergency numbers on hand, including the doctor's.

DO NOT:

* Bother to take a reading book or scan the TV schedule, as there will be no time to relax.

* Wear your best clothes. Whatever you wear will need to be washed thoroughly later.

* Take any money. Older children may invite you to play poker, and you'll be penniless in no time.

* Allow any of the grandchild's "friends" to enter the house, no matter what the excuse or explanation (it will be a conspiracy for sure).

The Real Truth

However conscientious you have been in your preparations for the evening's babysitting, there inevitably will be times when things do not go according to plan. When the parents return, you may have to come up with some plausible explanations. This handy guide should help.

The problem: None of the electricity in the house works.

GRANDPA'S EXPLANATION: "There was a heavy storm while you were out. I think the lightning must have done it."

THE REAL TRUTH: Grandpa overloaded the system by plugging his ancient projector into a socket shared with a table lamp to show off his photograph collection to his grandchild.

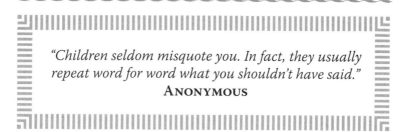

"Children seldom misquote you. In fact, they usually repeat word for word what you shouldn't have said."
ANONYMOUS

The problem: The grandchild's socks are soaking wet.

GRANDPA'S EXPLANATION: "He really wanted to help with the dishes."

THE REAL TRUTH: The grandchild took a dip in the dog's water dish while Grandpa was "dozing off for a moment."

The problem: Grandpa's socks are soaking wet.

GRANDPA'S EXPLANATION: "I took some trash out during the storm."

THE REAL TRUTH: The grandchild poured the dog's water into Grandpa's slippers when he was reading his paper.

The problem: The trash is full of daisies.

GRANDPA'S EXPLANATION: "I taught him the art of flower pressing."

THE REAL TRUTH: The grandchild and dog enjoyed a game of tug-of-war in the backyard while Grandpa was preparing lunch.

The problem: The remote control is missing.

GRANDPA'S EXPLANATION: "I haven't seen it at all! We didn't watch any TV."

THE REAL TRUTH: The remote is in the dishwasher, along with six toy cars and the remains of lunch.

The problem: The curtains won't close.

GRANDPA'S EXPLANATION: "I think that one of the curtain hooks snapped. Those plastic ones are very weak."

THE REAL TRUTH: Grandpa played a game of hide-and-seek and tangled his feet in the curtains when trying to escape.

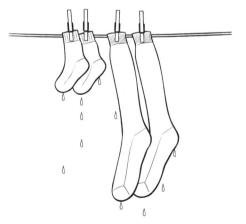

**The problem: The newspaper is stuck
to the kitchen table.**

GRANDPA'S EXPLANATION: "I've always told you not to have
sugar in your coffee — it makes such a sticky mess."

THE REAL TRUTH: Grandpa made a model car from cardboard
and superglue, but he forgot to clean up before reading his
paper afterward.

**The problem: The dog has a new bald patch
behind its left ear.**

GRANDPA'S EXPLANATION: "We noticed it scratching a lot —
perhaps you should take it to the vet in case it has fleas?"

THE REAL TRUTH: Some of the superglue dripped onto the
dog, so Grandpa had to give Fido a quick haircut.

TIP: If by some miracle the babysitting goes well, don't let the
parents know. Otherwise, before you know it, you could find
yourself in a more permanent situation!

Grandpa and School

*Grandson to Grandpa: "We've been asked
to bring something really old to school tomorrow.
Will you come with me?"*

Grandpas need to be aware of how the world has changed since their own school days and be sensitive to the fact that the new pressures on children can cause a lot of stress. Do try to get involved in the child's school life if possible, even if it's only to attend the child's school concert or play, or to supply some seedlings to sell at the school fair.

Grandparents "Needed in Schools"

Teachers can make use of the skills and experiences of retired grandparents as working parents struggle to find the time to get involved in their children's education. Grandparents can have a positive influence on pupils' behavior, motivation, and achievement in school. They have a wide range of experiences and skills to offer and they often have the time to share them with schoolchildren.

So what are you waiting for? Get involved!

Volunteer

One of the most popular ways that grandpas can help in school is by volunteering their time. Get in touch with your grandchild's school and find out if it needs volunteers to help in the classroom. Grandpas who take the plunge may quickly find themselves invited to join in other aspects of school life — from acting as a chaperone on field trips to cleaning out the class hamster's cage!

Grandparents' Day

Grandparents' Day is reserved for welcoming grandparents to their grandchildren's schools and for celebrating their relationships with their grandchildren. You might suggest these activities to your grandchild's school:

* **Grandparents go back to school:** Grandparents are invited to come into school to take part in lessons alongside their grandchildren. Sometimes they even have to wear the school uniform!

* **Grandparent interview:** Children plan a series of questions for their grandparents about what it was like when they were young.

* **Poems and stories:** Grandparents can be ideal subjects for a child's creative writing skills. Kids will enjoy describing their grandpa's looks, sayings, and mannerisms.

* **Variety show:** The children prepare a talent show, then perform for their grandparents.

* **Make a family tree:** Children must ask their parents and their grandparents about their past and present relatives and draw a family tree with their own name at the bottom on a large sheet of paper. You can continue the activity at home using the resources of the local library or by researching your descendants' records online.

* **Mapping "Nonna" and "Opa":** Children survey the ethnic origins of the members of the class and mark the countries on a world map. Students can research the words for "Grandpa" and "Grandma" in the various languages, using an online translation dictionary.

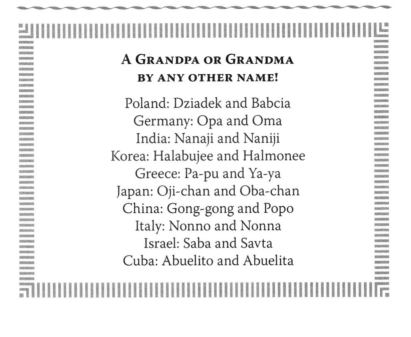

**A GRANDPA OR GRANDMA
BY ANY OTHER NAME!**

Poland: Dziadek and Babcia
Germany: Opa and Oma
India: Nanaji and Naniji
Korea: Halabujee and Halmonee
Greece: Pa-pu and Ya-ya
Japan: Oji-chan and Oba-chan
China: Gong-gong and Popo
Italy: Nonno and Nonna
Israel: Saba and Savta
Cuba: Abuelito and Abuelita

Grandpa, Can We . . . ?

Kids always come up with the best ideas for games. So the next time they say, "Grandpa, can we . . . ?," don't brush them off with the usual excuses. Instead, reply, "Sure! Why not?"

Grandpa, Can We Play Pirates?

"Ha-ha, me beauty, shiver me timbers!" All children seem to have a fascination with pirates, so a professional-quality "pirate voice" is an essential requisite of a good grandpa. Once you've got your grandchild in the mood, suggest the following activities:

Dress up as pirates

✳ Put on a striped T-shirt and tie a scarf at the neck.

✳ Tuck your pants into your socks.

* Make a big belt buckle out of cardboard covered with foil, or tie a scarf around your waist as a cummerbund.

* Tie a bandanna around your head and knot it at the back, or make a hat out of black paper and decorate it with a skull and crossbones drawn in chalk.

* Make a sword from cardboard, cover it in foil, and tuck it into your belt.

* Add a fake scar (use face paint or Grandma's mascara), a black eye patch, and an old brass curtain ring for an earring (attach it into the scarf or hat with a couple of stitches).

Make a pirate ship

You can make a basic ship for role playing from an upside-down table with some old sheets or curtains draped around it. Alternatively, you can use a very large cardboard box, with one of the sides trimmed down to allow access. Add a broomstick with another sheet or an old towel for a sail. Don't forget to make a Jolly Roger pirate flag with a skull and crossbones to go on top!

If you provide the basic props to inspire the children, you will find that they come up with their own ideas as they begin to play. Expect to make:

* Telescopes (use the tubes from paper towel rolls)

* A name tag for the ship

* A treasure map (if you stain it with cold tea, you can give it an ancient look)

* A treasure chest with "jewels" (make a trip to a second-hand store for some costume jewelry)

✳ A "sack" of gold pieces (small children will be content with aluminum foil–covered circles)

✳ A parrot (a cardboard cutout, painted or colored with markers)

✳ A plank

Of course, every good pirate will work up an appetite on the high seas, so prepare a good lunch after playing! How about making these Potato Pirate Ships to stay with the theme?

You will need:

1 large potato
2 tablespoons butter
2 mini hot dogs, cooked
2 slices of turkey lunch meat
2 toothpicks or small skewers
small can of baked beans

Preheat the oven to 400°F. Scrub and dry the potato, and prick all over with a fork. Place in the oven to bake for about 1 to

1½ hours. When the potato is soft, remove it from the oven and cut it in half lengthwise. Fluff each potato half with a fork and put 1 tablespoon of butter in each half. Spear one hot dog and then a rolled-up piece of turkey on each toothpick. Place one toothpick in each potato half with the turkey roll above the hot dog, like a sail and a flag. Heat the beans in a pan and arrange them around each potato, to represent the sea. Makes two potato pirate ships.

Grandpa, Can We Make a Greeting Card?

Encouraging your grandchildren to express their love to their close family is a great idea, so why not help them to construct personalized cards for special days and birthdays? A home-made effort really shows you care, and it will be treasured by its recipient.

Start by folding some brightly colored card stock in half. Help the child to write "Happy Father's Day" (or whatever the holiday) on the outside of the card in marker or crayon. Make sure you use different colors and maybe a template to make the letters look neat.

Now it's time to decorate the card. Choose a favorite theme that Dad will enjoy. For example, find out if your grandchild has been doing some gardening or playing football with Dad recently. Cut out pictures from magazines and stick them onto the card, or simply encourage the child to draw or paint his or her own design on the front.

Next comes the really important part: deciding on the words of the message. Maybe the child can write a poem that mentions some of the special things he or she has done with Dad during the past year. To make it extra personal, perhaps you could help to select some photographs to stick inside.

Grandpa, Can We Paint Our Faces?

This is a great activity for parties, but it's also fun to try at home if you're babysitting. Nontoxic face paints are inexpensive and easy to use, provided the "client" sits still.

Designs can be created to suit the occasion, so let your imagination run wild. Some ideas:

* A vampire

* A classic clown

* An animal face (puppy, tiger, panda, monkey, etc.)

* A butterfly

Grandpa, Can We Make a Kite?

To make a basic diamond kite, you will need:

* Two strong, straight wooden bamboo sticks, 35 and 40 inches in length

* Tape or glue

* Strong cord or string

* One sheet of strong paper or plastic tarp material for the cover (approximately 40 inches square)

* Ribbon bows

* Knife

Start by making a cross with the two sticks with the shorter stick placed horizontally at right angles across the longer one. Tape them together securely. Cut a notch deep enough for the cord to fit in at each end of both sticks (Grandpa should do this part). Take a long piece of cord and stretch it all the way around the

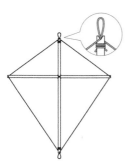

notches at each end of the kite frame as shown, making a little loop at both the top and bottom ends. Secure each cord by wrapping it around itself a few times in these places. The cord needs to be taut, but not so tight as to warp the sticks. Finish by cutting off what you don't need and securing the end with tape.

Lay the paper or plastic tarp material flat, and place the stick frame facedown on top of it. Trim the edges of the material to make the kite sail shape, leaving a slight overlap. Fold these edges over the string frame and tape or glue them down so that the material is taut.

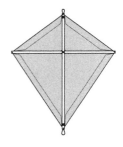

To make the kite's "bridle" (the string to which the flying line is attached), cut another piece of cord about 4 feet long. Tie one end to the loop at the top of the kite frame and the other end to the one at the bottom. Make another little loop just above the intersection of the crosspieces for the flying line to attach to. Make a tail by securing another piece of cord to the bottom of the kite and tying some ribbon bows at even intervals along its length.

Finally, tie a long piece of cord to the small loop in the middle of your kite's bridle and you are ready to fly!

Grandpa, Can We Make a Pair of Stilts?

This is a fun project for older children to help with, but it does require some general woodworking skills. Once you've built the stilts, be sure to closely supervise any children who use them.

You will need:

* Two pieces of wood about 6 inches in length and roughly 2 inches thick

* Two pieces of wood 5 feet in length and roughly 2 inches thick

* Wood glue

* Four each of bolts, nuts, and washers

* Sandpaper

* Clear varnish

* Heavy tape

* Drill (always use proper safety precautions and never let a child handle the drill)

To make each stilt, attach a small piece of wood 8 to 12 inches from the end of a longer piece, using glue and a bolt. Sand and varnish the stilts. Wrap some tape around the top of each stilt to make a handgrip. Make sure you supply your grandchild with a helmet and kneepads whenever he or she uses the stilts! A good way of learning to walk with stilts is to step onto the footrests from a box or raised platform of roughly the same height, rather than climbing onto them from the ground.

Grandpa, Can We Make a Clown Mask?

You will need:

∗ Some plain white cardboard or card stock

∗ A pencil and paints

∗ Scissors

∗ Brightly colored fuzzy fabric

∗ Glue

∗ A length of elastic

Start by marking the outline of the clown's face on the cardboard and draw where the eyes, nose, and mouth holes will be, based on the size of your grandchild's face. Use the scissors to cut around the face and carefully cut out the holes. Encourage your grandchild to help you paint the face, and remember to add a huge smile! Cut some strips of the bright fabric and glue some to each side to create hair. Finally, make a little hole near each side and thread a length of elastic through the holes. Tie off the elastic so that the child can wear the mask.

Grandpa, Can We Watch a Movie?

A trip to the movies — with the prospect of popcorn and soda — is an attractive possibility for both Grandpa and grandchild. Use the newspaper or Internet to find a film that's suitable for the child's age. If there's nothing at your local theater, you can set up your own "home movie" experience with a DVD, dimmed lights, and a bowl of homemade popcorn. Escorting your grandchild to his or her seat by flashlight is optional! Of course there are hundreds of films you could choose, but here are a few options. Be sure to check with the child's parents first to clear your movie selection with them.

* *Mr. Magorium's Wonder Emporium* is about an amazing toy store where everything comes to life. Dustin Hoffman is the eccentric proprietor. It's a colorful film with slapstick comedy and gadgets galore!

* *Fred Claus* gives a fun insight into Santa's family, with startling special effects. Santa's Christmas preparations are jeopardized by the antics of his rascal brother, Fred Claus.

* *Bee Movie* is an animated film about talking bees! It has a great adventure plot for the kids, and Jerry Seinfeld's witty humor will entertain Grandpa.

* *The Chronicles of Narnia* is a series of movies based on C. S. Lewis's fantasy novels.

* The *Harry Potter* films are superb entertainment, though the later films are only for older children.

* The *High School Musical* series is similarly unmissable, and it's especially popular with granddaughters!

Grandpa, Can We Do Some Cooking?

Encouraging your grandchildren to enjoy cooking their own food gives them a great start in life and fosters healthy eating habits. These recipes are simple enough for even the youngest child to help with.

Grandpa's Pizza Express

Everyone knows that you can order a pizza for delivery, but making your own is something else! Of course, the easiest way to do this is to buy ready-made crusts and experiment by adding favorite toppings, such as mushrooms, peppers, cooked meat, pineapple, olives, etc. It's a good way to introduce children to new tastes. Remember to brush the base with olive oil first and add some tomato sauce and grated mozzarella cheese. Bake in a preheated oven at 425°F for 15 to 20 minutes.

If you're feeling more ambitious, why not make your own simple dough? To make dough for one large pizza, you will need:

2½ ounces lukewarm water
1 teaspoon sugar
1½ teaspoons active dry yeast
1 cup flour
1 teaspoon salt
1 egg, beaten
olive oil

Whisk the water and sugar together in a bowl, sprinkle the yeast on top, and leave for about 15 minutes, until the mixture becomes frothy. Sift the flour and salt into a bowl, pour in the yeast mixture, and add the beaten egg. Mix to a fairly stiff doughlike consistency, adding a little more water if necessary. Place the dough on a lightly floured board and knead for about

10 minutes. Cover the dough with plastic wrap or a damp cloth and put in a warm place for about an hour to rise.

Next, give the dough another light knead, then put it on a greased baking sheet and flatten it to form a large circle. Brush with olive oil and add your preferred choice of topping, then bake as directed on page 91.

Cream Cheese Brownies

To make approximately 16 brownies, you will need:

¾ cup flour
1 teaspoon baking powder
8 ounces cream cheese
3 eggs
¼ cup granulated sugar
1 teaspoon pure vanilla extract
4 ounces dark (bittersweet) chocolate
8 tablespoons unsalted butter
¾ cup brown sugar
1 tablespoon milk, warmed
8-inch square baking pan
or 10-inch-diameter round pan

Preheat the oven to 325°F. Grease the baking pan and dust it with flour or line it with nonstick parchment paper. Sift the flour and baking powder together in a bowl.

To make the cheese mixture, beat the cream cheese in a bowl until soft and smooth. Add 1 egg, the granulated sugar, and vanilla extract, and beat until all the ingredients are well blended.

Gently melt the chocolate and butter together in a heatproof bowl placed over a pan of simmering water. Remove from the heat, stir, then add the brown sugar. Beat in the remaining 2 eggs and gently stir in the flour and baking powder mixture you prepared earlier.

Spread two-thirds of the brownie mixture over the bottom of the baking pan. Add the warm milk to the remaining brownie mixture and stir until the consistency becomes the same as that of the cream cheese mixture.

Spoon the cream cheese in little heaps on top of the mixture in the pan, then spoon on the remaining brownie mixture in between the cream cheese. Using a fork, swirl the brownie and cream cheese toppings together.

Bake for 30 to 35 minutes, or until the brownie mixture is just set in the center. Leave to cool in the pan, then cut it into squares and remove carefully.

Ice Cream Sodas

This is a really fun dessert that's more of a chemical reaction than a recipe, really.

You will need:

A selection of fruit, such as peaches,
    strawberries, and raspberries
Ice cream (vanilla
    or a fruity flavor
    works best)
Sparkling lemonade
Tall glasses

Cut the fruit into pieces and fill up about a quarter of each glass with a layer of the fruit mixture. Use an ice cream scoop to add a "bomb" of ice cream to each glass. Pour the lemonade over the ice cream and watch it fizz!

Home and Away

Some grandpas are lucky: They live close by, and interaction with their grandchildren is easy and regular. But mobility is greater these days, and many families live farther apart. As a result, more grandfathers live a long distance away from their relatives — perhaps even on different continents!

However, technology is making the world smaller every day, and enthusiastic grandpas can harness these tools to overcome distance and enjoy close contact as their grandchildren grow.

Telephone: Phone calls are always special because they're interactive, and the exchange of news is so immediate. Evening and weekend calls are often free for "family and friends." Try to establish a regular time to talk.

Text: Cool grandpas will use their cell phones to text. It's a great method for sharing firsthand experiences, and you can use it to consult with your grandchild on daily decisions. Pictures or downloaded music may even be attached!

Photographs: Grandpas are often sent lots of photographs of their grandchildren, but it's equally important for Grandpa to send photographs of *his* activities and successes to the grandchildren. For example, "Grandpa wins local darts tournament," or "Here's the new patio Grandpa just built!"

Video: Special events are best recorded this way, from those magical first steps to the first time your grandchild scores a winning goal for the soccer team.

Postal exchanges: "Snail mail" is slow, yes, but letters written by hand feel special; greeting cards can be made and sent; and gifts can be exchanged by mail as well.

E-mail: Many teenagers routinely use e-mail every day, so why not get on the same wavelength? E-mail is free if you already have a broadband connection, and it also allows you to attach photographs and videos. Remember, too, that keeping in touch need not simply be a matter of swapping mundane information about your life. A fortunate grandpa will find some common interest with his grandchild — a sports team you both support or an activity you both enjoy, such as movies or fishing — and use e-mail to send interesting information about it found on the Internet. E-mailing each other about a "joint project" in the area of interest can be really fulfilling. For example, organizing a camping trip or supplying snippets of trivia about a TV show.

Long-distance games: Playing chess or similar games with each other via the Internet can be relaxing and will add an additional competitive dimension to the relationship.

Networking sites: Another Web method offering easy access to each other — and the wider family — is to use a social networking site such as Facebook. Ask your grandchild to tell you how it works!

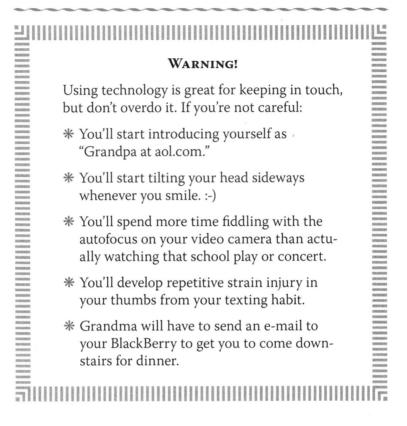

WARNING!

Using technology is great for keeping in touch, but don't overdo it. If you're not careful:

✳ You'll start introducing yourself as "Grandpa at aol.com."

✳ You'll start tilting your head sideways whenever you smile. :-)

✳ You'll spend more time fiddling with the autofocus on your video camera than actually watching that school play or concert.

✳ You'll develop repetitive strain injury in your thumbs from your texting habit.

✳ Grandma will have to send an e-mail to your BlackBerry to get you to come downstairs for dinner.

Planning the Special Visit

Regular contact makes planning a "special visit" so much easier and more exciting to anticipate. When Grandpa does "fly over" or "drive across," it will be with a clear purpose in mind, such as watching the grandchild's favorite musical or building that model aircraft. This is a great way of building a close relationship, even if circumstances have forced you far apart.

A Rainy Day

The clouds loom overhead and the sky opens. It's a rainy day, and the kids are trapped inside. The afternoon stretches ahead blankly. Boredom soon sets in, and tempers start to fray. What on earth can Grandpa do to amuse and distract the little darlings?

Being prepared with a selection of "quiet games" is an invaluable quality in a grandfather, and it's likely to result in a shower of appreciation from the parents. These types of games can calm children, but they can also be stimulating and encourage cooperation and sharing. Many of the following games can be equally valuable during a car trip.

Here is the ultimate "Survivor's Guide to the Rainy Day."

Magic Numbers

Grandpa claims to be a mind reader! Tell your grandchild to think of a number, but keep it to him- or herself. Then tell your grandchild to double the number, add ten, and divide by two. Then instruct him or her to subtract the number he or she first chose.

Now place a finger to your grandchild's temple and stare into his or her "mind." Finally, announce that the answer is five.

When you're asked to repeat this amazing trick, ask your grandchild to add six instead of ten. The answer will be three.

Got My Number?

For each player, draw two grids of ten by ten squares (using a separate piece of paper for each one). Mark the horizontal squares from A to J, and mark the vertical squares from 1 to 10. Each square thus has its own coordinates (for example, C3 or F6).

Each player now secretly marks the shape of a number on one of the grids by shading in a selection of squares. The players take turns calling the coordinates of a square to each other, and the opponent must say that it is a "miss" or a "hit." A "hit" occurs when the one player selects one of the shaded squares on another's hidden grid.

Each player keeps a record of his or her guesses by marking the squares they have guessed on the second grid. The game is won when one player is able to guess the other's number based on the number of shaded squares he or she has "hit."

Word Game

For each player, draw a grid with a number of columns and rows. The first column is for "groups," and the top row is for "letters." You can choose as many columns/rows as time (and space on the paper) allows, but make sure each player ends up with the same-size grid.

Players take turns choosing groups, which are then written in the first column on everyone's grids, one beneath the other. Groups could be things like names of football teams, trees, colors, cars, types of furniture, etc. Once all the groups have been filled in, the game can begin.

A letter is chosen by opening a book to any page, closing your eyes, and using a pencil to randomly point to a letter. The letter is written in the top row of column 2. Let's say the letter is *S*. In the next three minutes, players must find a word beginning with *S* for each of the groups. For example:

Groups	Letter *S*
Football teams	Steelers
Trees	Spruce
Color	Silver
Cars	Suzuki
Furniture	Sofa

At the end of three minutes, each player reads out his or her answers. You get one point for each original answer, but if two or more players have the same answer, they don't get any points for it. At the end of an agreed-upon number of rounds, scores are added up, and the winner is announced!

Hangman

This old favorite is almost certainly a game you played in your own childhood, but do you remember how to play it?

First, one person is chosen to be the "hangman." He or she selects a word (let's say the word is *rhythm*). The word has six letters, so six dashes will be made like this on a piece of paper:

— — — — — —

The other players have to guess a letter, one at a time, and if the letter features in the word, the hangman has to mark it on the paper. So, for example, if the first guess is *T*, then the paper would look like this:

$$— \ — \ — \ \underline{T} \ — \ —$$

If the letter guessed is not in the word, however, then the first line of the gallows can be drawn.

Letters that have been guessed are listed underneath the gallows so that the guessers don't repeat them.

The game is finished if:

* The guessers figure out the word (they can try a guess at any time, but if they are wrong, another line is drawn on the gallows). Whoever guesses correctly becomes the hangman and chooses the word in the next round.

* The gallows are completed before the word is guessed, in which case the hangman has won and gets to choose the next word again.

Who Am I?

The first person decides the name of a famous person he or she is going to "be." For example, Madonna, Santa Claus, or Shakespeare. The person does not reveal the name, but just says "Ready" when he or she has thought of someone.

The other players take turns asking questions — but they can receive only a yes or no in reply. For example, "Are you dead?" or "Are you fictional?" Each player can continue asking questions as long as he or she receives a yes in reply. If the answer is no, then it's the next player's turn to start guessing.

Good questions will narrow down the options:

"Are you male?" — YES

Are you alive?" — YES

"Are you famous?" — YES

"Are you American?" — YES

"Are you an athlete?" — YES

"Are you a baseball player?" — YES

"Are you Derek Jeter?" — YES

From Number One Crompton with No Bromptons

This is a tongue twister and memory game. The players sit in a circle and are numbered off: "Number One Crompton," "Number Two Crompton," etc.

All players start with "No Bromptons" (don't worry, this will start to make sense in a minute!).

The first player starts the game by selecting another player and saying, "From Number One Crompton with No Bromptons to Number Two Crompton with No Bromptons." The words must be said clearly and accurately with no hesitation or error. If an error of any kind is made, then the player gets a "brompton."

If this happened to Number One Crompton, he would have to restart by saying, "From Number One Crompton with ONE Brompton to Number Two Crompton with No Bromptons." The player who is addressed in this way then has to pick some-one else in turn.

Players have to concentrate — the game gets harder as more mistakes are made and players have to remember each person's score. Players can be eliminated if they get ten bromptons, or a time limit can be set for each round, until the eventual winner emerges.

This game can be made more fun by substituting your own surname/nonsense word in place of Crompton/Bromptons. For example, you could use Dixon/Flixons or Stewart/Chewarts.

Consequences

There are two versions of this game. The first is the word version, in which each player is given a sheet of paper. Grandpa asks each player to write down the name of a male person at the top of the paper: for example, "Mr. Plod, the policeman," or "Bill Clinton," or "Tom Cruise."

Once players have selected and written down a name, they fold the paper over so that the name cannot be seen, and they pass on their paper to the person to their left.

Now Grandpa says, "And he met . . . ," and everyone has to write the name of a female: for example, "Margaret Thatcher," "Alice in Wonderland," or "the girl next door."

Once again the paper is folded and passed on, and the game continues with the following categories:

* Where? (The name of an unusual place is written.)

* What did he say to her? (A funny phrase is chosen.)

* What did she say to him? (A reply is written.)

* What was the consequence? (Some event or action is selected.)

* And the world said? (A "judgment" or "moral comment" is written.)

Papers are now unfolded and each person reads out the resulting script. Here's a funny example:

Grandpa
met: Margaret Thatcher
in: the bathroom
He said to her: "Would you like to dance?"
She said to him: "Don't be ridiculous!"
The consequence was: He was imprisoned for fifty years.
And the world said: "Age before beauty!"

The second version of the game Consequences also involves a piece of paper folded over and passed on to the next player. This time, each player draws a section of a body of an animal or person, starting with the head, then the body, then the legs, and then the feet. When the paper is unfolded at the end, a "monster" is revealed!

I Went into a Store and Bought . . .

This is a fun memory game for three or more players. Start by sitting in a circle. The first person chooses an item and says, "I went into a store and bought [for example] a green umbrella."

The second person says, "I went into a store and bought a green umbrella and a bag of potatoes."

The third person says, "I went into a store and bought a green umbrella, a bag of potatoes, and a bunch of yellow daffodils."

The list goes on and on until a player forgets one of the items purchased and is eliminated. The winner is the player who doesn't make a mistake and can remember the whole list!

Kim's Game

This is another memory game popular with young children, and is featured in Rudyard Kipling's novel *Kim*.

Assemble a group of miscellaneous objects on a large tray. You will need about ten different objects. Some suggested items are a spoon, a pencil, a tomato, and a television remote control.

The tray is shown to the children for a few moments. Grandpa then covers the tray with a cloth and secretly removes one or more of the objects. Now the tray can be unveiled again, and the children have to identify which object (or objects) have been removed. It can be harder than it seems!

Teen Traumas

The teenage years are viewed with apprehension and awe by parents. This is the age of puberty and rebellion, when raging hormones cause wild mood swings, tears, and tantrums. It is also a time when independence from parents is the child's unstated goal.

Ironically, grandparents often find that their role grows in value for their grandchildren during this phase. A grandfather can be the independent adult, the source of impartial advice, a listening ear, and a comforting shoulder. He can be consulted about the pressures of adolescence and he can provide a welcome "safe haven" when it all gets to be too much.

However, a good relationship between teenage grandchild and grandfather starts with you keeping the relationship proactive. You can't expect to be trusted to act as a counselor about the child's issues if you haven't been positively interacting with him or her throughout his or her childhood.

How to do it?

Don't forget that teenagers are kids who are still learning and making mistakes.

And don't forget that they think they're adults and consequently require respect for their decisions, even when you disagree with them!

"A boy becomes an adult three years before his parents think he does, and about two years after he thinks he does."
LEWIS B. HERSHEY, U.S. Army general

The most important thing you can do with your grandchildren at this age is to spend some time with them. However, this might be trickier than it used to be, as their own social lives become busier. Here are a few activity suggestions.

Let's Go to the Movies

Keep up the good habit of watching films together if you can. Going to the movies can be a bonding experience for Grandpa and the teenage grandchild. It's not expensive, and it's an easy way to stimulate conversation and discussion about issues of importance.

Grandpa the Counselor

*"The young always have the same problem —
how to rebel and conform at the same time.
They have now solved this by defying
their parents and copying one another."*
QUENTIN CRISP, author

It can be difficult to talk to teenagers when they withdraw into a surly or uncommunicative mood. The trick is to choose something that interests them, so finding a shared hobby is ideal. Once you've found this common ground, you'll see that talking about other issues follows naturally.

If you spend a lot of time with your teenage grandchild, you're more likely to fall into discussion and be implicitly invited to act as an informal counselor. Here are some issues that may arise.

✳ Smoking, drinking, and taking drugs

✳ Underage sex and contraception

✳ Arguments with Mom and Dad

✳ Bullying at school

✳ Membership in a "gang" of friends

✳ Nighttime curfew

✳ Boyfriends or girlfriends

* How to keep their bedrooms tidy

* Whether to attend college and/or where to attend college

How can you prepare for all this? The recipe is the same no matter what the issue.

* Listen first and show understanding, empathy, and respect.

* Provide information, or suggest other reliable information sources.

* Don't exceed your own expertise. If you aren't sure how to respond, tell your grandchild you'll do some research and will get back to him or her.

* Maintain strict confidentiality.

* Don't express a view unless you're specifically asked for one. Then choose your words carefully.

* Encourage your grandchild to share concerns and decisions with his or her parents and explain why this is a good idea.

* Encourage your grandchild to think and act independently and not to conform automatically to group pressures.

* Ensure that you convey the message that you care about your grandchild no matter what, even if you express concern about his or her behavior.

"Little children, headache; big children, heartache."
ITALIAN PROVERB

What Grandpa Meant to Say

One of the things that children always notice about their grandpas is the strange language they often use. Being from a different generation, grandpas are the repositories of past expressions and often allude to events or experiences that have been clouded by the mists of time. Grandpas can baffle and perhaps unwittingly offend others by using some of these expressions. The following examples serve to warn grandpas of the risks and to provide others with a translation of the meaning Grandpa intended.

GRANDPA-SPEAK: *"There you go again, Grandma, you old battle-ax."*
EXPLANATION: This term has been used for a belligerent, domineering older woman since the fourteenth century. Its misogynistic connotations were subverted in recent years when *The Battle Axe* was chosen as the title of a women's rights magazine.

GRANDPA-SPEAK: *"Quiet down, my dear. We don't want to air our dirty laundry in public."*
EXPLANATION: The expression means to keep family faults private, and not to publicize them. It may have arisen from a French proverb used in a speech by Napoleon on his return from Elba. ("It is at home — not in public — that one washes one's dirty linen.")

GRANDPA-SPEAK: *"That will be the acid test of your affection for me!"*

EXPLANATION: This means the ultimate test. Nitric acid (aquafortis) was used in the Middle Ages as the way of judging the worth of gold.

GRANDPA-SPEAK: *"You're driving balls to the wall today. Slow down!"*

EXPLANATION: This expression has nothing to do with private parts. Instead, it is said to have originated with fighter plane aviation. The "balls" were the knobs of the aircraft's throttle control, so "balls to the wall" means pushing the throttle all the way forward and going at full speed.

GRANDPA-SPEAK: *"Well, I'll be a monkey's uncle!"*

EXPLANATION: This expression of disbelief was originally a sarcastic remark made by those who didn't believe in Charles Darwin's theory of evolution.

GRANDPA-SPEAK: *"Brrr! It's cold enough to freeze the balls off a brass monkey this morning!"*

EXPLANATION: Surprisingly, there is a theory that this phrase is not an anatomical one. It's said that the "brass monkey" on a sailing ship was a brass plate that secured the cannonballs. When the weather was too cold, the brass contracted and the cannonballs were in danger of rolling free. The theory has never been proven true, though.

GRANDPA-SPEAK: *"Oh, I got shivers down my spine. Spiderwebs give me the willies."*

EXPLANATION: In Slavic folklore, the *wilis* were the restless spirits of young girls who died before they married (as in the ballet *Giselle*). It is now taken to mean something upsetting and disturbing.

GRANDPA-SPEAK: *"I've upset your grandma again! 'Hell hath no fury like a woman scorned.'"*

EXPLANATION: This is a common misquotation. The original lines, by William Congreve in his play *The Mourning Bride* (1697), are as follows: "Heav'n has no Rage like Love to Hatred turn'd/ Nor Hell a Fury like a Woman scorn'd."

Did You Know?

Being a grandpa is becoming more and more popular! Demographic trends show that as we are living longer, more men are now grandfathers than ever before. But did you know the following facts and figures?

✳ In the United States, there are sixty million grandparents. Five percent of all children under eighteen live in a grandparent's home.

✳ Since the 1950s, life expectancy has increased by eight to ten years. That is an increase of two years in life expectancy every decade. In other words, for every hour we live, we add twelve minutes to our life expectancy.

✳ By the age of fifty-four, one in every two people is a grandparent.

✳ Grandparents on average have 4.4 grandchildren.

✳ More than one-third of grandparents under the age of sixty still have a dependent child living at home.

✳ In the past two generations, the percent of grandparents caring for grandchildren has jumped from 33 percent to 82 percent, with more than a third of grandparents spending the equivalent of three days a week caring for their grandchildren.

The Record Holders

Becoming a grandpa for the first time is a surefire way to make yourself feel instantly old. But look at what all of these men have accomplished in their old age!

Grandpa or Dad?

By the age of thirty, more than 50 percent of men have fathered a child. In 2004, about twenty-four in every thousand men aged forty to forty-four fathered a child, which is up 18 percent from ten years prior. If that doesn't put a spring in your step, perhaps this will: The world's oldest new dad is a grandfather named Nanu Ram Jogi, who hails from the Indian state of Rajasthan. In August 2007, at the age of ninety, he fathered his latest child. He cannot remember how many children he has already had with his four wives, but he estimates he has twelve sons, nine daughters, and at least twenty grandchildren.

The oldest man on Everest

In May 2008, a seventy-six-year-old Nepalese man reportedly became the oldest person to climb to the summit of Mount Everest. In achieving this goal, he broke the record set by a seventy-one-year-old Japanese teacher one year prior.

The oldest heavyweight champ

Boxer George Foreman was twice the world heavyweight champion (1973–74 and 1994–95). When he regained the title at age forty-five, he became the oldest world heavyweight champion ever.

George Foreman has ten children and numerous grandchildren. Each of his five sons is named George, which is a unique way of getting around the problem most grandpas have of forgetting their children's names.

The oldest racing driver

According to the *Guinness Book of World Records*, actor and grandfather Paul Newman became the oldest-ever racing driver in 2005, when, at the age of eighty, he competed in the Rolex 24 at Daytona.

The oldest U.S. president

Ronald Reagan (1911–2004) was elected at age sixty-nine in 1980, and became the oldest U.S. president. He survived being seriously wounded in an assassination attempt, and was then elected to a second term in office — by the time he finished this term, he was seventy-seven years old. Before becoming president, Reagan was a radio host, an actor in film and television, and governor of California.

The oldest bank robber

J. L. Hunter Rountree was sentenced to more than twelve years in prison in 2004 after pleading guilty to stealing $1,999 from a Texas bank the previous year. He was ninety-one at the time. Rountree said he staged his first robbery when he was eighty-six to take revenge against banks for sending him into a financial crisis. He never had to serve his time in prison, though, because he died soon after his sentencing.

The oldest sportsman

Swedish marksman Oscar Swahn became the oldest Olympic gold medal winner when he won the deer-shooting event at the 1912 Olympics at the age of sixty-four.

Some Extraordinary Grandpas

All at sea

A pair of grandfathers attempting to row across the Atlantic Ocean had to be rescued just nine days into their trip. Jerry Rogers, fifty-seven, and Keith Oliver, fifty-three, were 340 miles into their 2,975-mile voyage in November 2005 when they had to activate the emergency beacon. Their problem was a malfunction with the water maker on their boat, *Bright Spark*. Had they been successful, they would have been the oldest crew to row across the Atlantic Ocean.

Grandpa seeks family!

A retired, widowed Italian teacher, Giorgio Angelozzi, took out an advertisement in a national newspaper pleading for a family to adopt him as a grandfather. He claimed he was lonely following the death of his wife in 1992. People across the world took pity on him, and he was inundated with offers. He moved in with a family in northern Italy who opened their hearts to him, but then he disappeared, leaving a trail of debts behind him. It turned out he had a criminal record stretching back to the 1960s, and he had never even been a teacher.

Lucky escapes

Belfast chef Melvyn Goldberger was amazed to discover that both his grandfathers had cheated death in different countries, miles apart. One was saved from the *Titanic* when he was fortuitously (as it turns out) struck down with appendicitis twenty minutes before the vessel sailed on her ill-fated maiden voyage. The other — his paternal grandfather — managed to escape death on Kristallnacht: By good fortune, one of the guards who arrested him that night was an old school friend who let him slip away instead of sending him to certain death in a concentration camp.

Grandpa's Changing Role

Grandparents in all societies are important members of the family. In traditional Asian cultures, for example, respect for and obedience to the grandparent is very important: Grandparents usually exercise authority in family matters, and their descendants are expected to obey their seniors without question. For many years in the West, grandparents enjoyed similar status in the extended family, with a direct and clear role in relation to the care and nurture of children. Yet we live in changing times, and the situation of many grandparents has shifted in the past fifty years. With industrialization, greater social mobility, and the trend for smaller nuclear families, some members of the older generation have found themselves marginalized and isolated from their families. Many others, however, have found that they now play an invaluable part in keeping the family together, providing affordable child care for the increasing number of women who go back to work after having children. If you fall into this latter group, count yourself lucky — it may be hard work sometimes, but you can become a huge influence on your grandchild's life. You can also have the pleasure of watching him or her grow and learn.

"Nobody can do for little children what grandparents do. Grandparents sort of sprinkle stardust over the lives of little children."
ALEX HALEY, author

Grandparents and Parents

GRANDPARENTS: The people who think your children are wonderful even though they're sure you're not raising them right.

Caring for your grandchild on a regular basis can be a hugely beneficial arrangement for you, the parents, and the grandchild. Both younger generations will benefit from your wisdom and experience, and your ability to bring a mature perspective to the ups and downs of family life is invaluable. Being "one step removed" from the child means that you are more likely to keep calm when things become fraught (if your grandchild is a toddler or teen, you'll understand!). You may even find the child tends to behave much better with you than with his or her own parents. However, it's important not to undermine the parents in any way, so a good grandpa is smart enough to realize that he must be subtle and sensitive in "sharing" his expertise.

The rules of the game

FOR GRANDPARENTS:

✳ Learn and honor the "house rules" that the parents have established. Never overrule the parents' decisions about how they choose to raise their children.

✳ If you have any concerns about the way the parents are managing your grandchildren, air them only at appropriate confidential moments.

✳ Encourage the grandchildren to understand and respect all that their parents do for them.

FOR PARENTS:

✳ Try to foster a good grandparent-grandchild relationship. Always speak of the children's grandparents affectionately, even if you don't always see eye to eye with your parents or in-laws.

✳ It's a good idea to make a point of discussing your "house rules" with the grandparents so that you have a mutual understanding of what is expected (and so that you can put up a united front for the children).

✳ That said, try to allow some flexibility when your children are visiting their grandparents. It's not the end of the world if they're allowed to stay up past their usual bedtime or if they are given some money to buy candy.

✳ However, if the grandparents consistently undermine you with regard to your children, try to sit down with them calmly to discuss the problem. Often it is simply a breakdown of communication or a desire to indulge a much-loved grandchild rather than anything malicious at work.

Hunky Grandpa

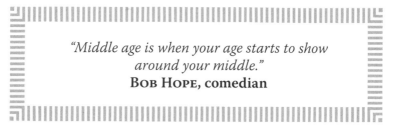
Grandfathers have an image problem. Ask the kids at school about grandfathers, and they will mention sweaters and false teeth. These are not cool. Sorry, Grandpa, but they're not. So how do you "get hip with the kids" and make yourself trendy in their eyes? What you need is a grandpa makeover.

Stocktaking

Most grandpas have accumulated their wardrobe over time and collected their toiletries in a similar way. So an inventory review is the first stage of your grand makeover. Perhaps find your oldest aftershave and throw out any clothes that don't fit or you haven't worn in a year. Get your family on board to help you be ruthless (though not *too* ruthless — you want to be left with at least one pair of underwear and pants to wear). Remember, if you're unsure, toss it! Or even better, in these ecologically friendly times, take it to the local thrift store or recycle it.

OUT!

* Velour slippers

* "Comfortable" sneakers

* Shirts with frayed cuffs and collars

* Any old pipes and smoking paraphernalia

* Old shoes with worn-out soles

* Odd or holey socks

* "Lucky" underwear

* Little toiletry bottles "appropriated" from hotels

IN!

* New underwear — some boxers or classic briefs

* A formal suit and "stylish" tie

* A crisp white shirt

* A pair of good-quality leather shoes

* A pair of well-fitted sneakers

* A pair of jeans

* Leather gloves

* Leather slippers

* Hiking boots

* A dental checkup (with a whitening treatment)

* A "manscape" at the barbershop: a trim for the head, ears, and nose

* An exercise routine

* An eye-catching watch — even if it's not Rolex or Cartier!

* A cell phone or PDA (personal digital assistant)

Some Hunky Grandpas

Frank Sinatra

Imagine having "the Chairman of the Board" as your grandpa! Born in 1915, Frank Sinatra had a charmed career as swing singer, pop star, and actor. He was always the man about town — as a member of the infamous Rat Pack and through his contact with politicians and his alleged ties to organized crime. Sinatra had three children — Nancy, Frank Jr., and Tina — with his first wife, Nancy Barbato. He was subsequently married three more times, to the actresses Ava Gardner and Mia Farrow, and finally to Barbara Marx.

Clint Eastwood

Born in 1930, this legendary American film director, producer, and actor has been married twice and has five daughters and two sons by five different women. He was in his sixties when he fathered his last two children, and his grandchildren are actually older than his youngest child, Morgan! He once said, "I like to joke that since my children weren't making me any grandchildren, I had two of my own. It is a terrific feeling being a dad again at my age."

Paul Newman

Award-winning actor and film director, philanthropist, and salad dressing magnate, Paul Newman was no ordinary grandpa. With eight grandchildren from his five daughters (he also had a son who died young), this Academy Award–winning grandpa was regarded as one of the world's sexiest men until his death in 2008.

Mick Jagger

Still wiggling those snakelike hips well into his sixties, this Rolling Stone has been a member of one of the world's greatest rock 'n' roll bands for more than four decades. With seven children and numerous grandchildren, Jagger is still famous for his high-profile relationships with women and, as yet, still has no plans to retire from touring. Way to go, Grandpa!

Grandpa and Grandma

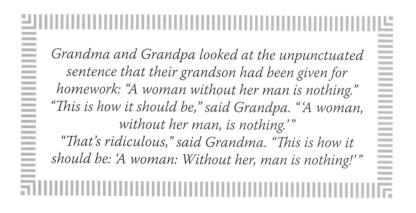

Grandma and Grandpa looked at the unpunctuated sentence that their grandson had been given for homework: "A woman without her man is nothing." "This is how it should be," said Grandpa. "'A woman, without her man, is nothing.'" "That's ridiculous," said Grandma. "This is how it should be: 'A woman: Without her, man is nothing!'"

In these modern times when divorce is on the rise and the institution of marriage is in decline, grandparents can perhaps teach a thing or two to the younger generation about the secrets of marital harmony.

Mileposts Along the Journey of Bliss

One important expectation for Grandpa is to remember the date of his wedding anniversary and to choose the appropriate present. This shows that he appreciates the many years of bliss he has enjoyed with Grandma. Modern grandpas make sure they have programmed their cell phone *and* their computer calendar with alerts and alarms at least two weeks before the date.

The following chart is a valuable reference for generating suitable ideas for gifts. And never underestimate this sage advice: The best way to remember your anniversay is to forget it once!

Anniversary	Gift
20th	China
25th	Silver
30th	Pearl
35th	Coral
40th	Ruby
45th	Sapphire
50th	Gold
55th	Emerald
60th	Diamond

Birthdays, too, are important milestones that a grandpa misses at his peril. After all, the definition of a diplomat is a man who remembers a woman's birthday but forgets her age. If you do make the ultimate faux pas and forget to buy her a present, a little smooth talking should help. What grandma wouldn't melt if you say, "How do you expect me to remember your birthday when you never look any older, my darling?"

"When a man has a birthday, he may take a day off. When a woman has one, she takes off at least a year."
ANONYMOUS

A Sense of Humor

Ask any couple of long standing and they will tell you: The secret of a happy marriage is a sense of humor. This involves the ability of Grandpa and Grandma to laugh at themselves and each other, whatever life may throw at them.

Gender roles of grandparents are often distinct and offer rich material for jokes and laughter, which are the cement of affection and love. See if the following make you both smile.

The wisdom of age

* A successful man is one who makes more money than his wife can spend. A successful woman is one who can find such a man.

* To be happy with a man, you must understand him a lot and love him a little. To be happy with a woman, you must love her a lot and not try to understand her at all.

* Husbands: Only two things are necessary to keep one's wife happy. One is to let her think she is having her way, and the other is to let her have it.

* Any married man should forget his mistakes. There's no use in two people remembering the same thing.

* Grandchildren are God's rewards for not killing your own children.

Do you remember when?

Grandma and Grandpa were sitting in their rocking chairs watching a beautiful sunset. Grandma turned to Grandpa with a twinkle in her eye and said, "Do you remember when we first started dating and you used to just casually reach over and take my hand?"

Grandpa smiled knowingly, looked over at her, and took her aged hand in his.

Grandma sighed and then reminisced, "And do you remember how, after we were engaged, you'd sometimes lean over and suddenly kiss me on the cheek?"

Grandpa dutifully leaned slowly toward Grandma and gave her a lingering kiss on her wrinkled cheek.

Growing bolder still, Grandma said, "Darling, do you remember how, after we were first married, you'd love to snuggle close and nibble my ear?"

Grandpa slowly rose from his rocker and headed into the house.

Disappointed, Grandma called after him, "Where are you going?"

Grandpa replied, "To get my teeth!"

Out of the mouths of babes

A little boy says, "Daddy, Daddy, I want to get married!"

The father smiles and replies, "For that, son, you need to find a lady."

The son says, "I've found a lady — my grandma."

"Let me get this straight," the father says. "You want to marry my mother? You can't do that!"

"Why not?" the son says. "You married mine!"

Know when to keep your mouth shut

Every year, Grandpa and Grandma went to the summer fair. Every year, Grandpa would say, "I'd really like to go for a ride in

that stunt plane." And every year, Grandma would respond by saying, "I'd like to go for a ride in that plane, too, but the ride costs fifty dollars, and fifty dollars is fifty dollars!"

Finally, Grandpa got up the courage and said, "Grandma, I'm seventy-eight years old. If I don't ride that stunt plane this year, I may never get another chance."

Once again, Grandma said, "That ride costs fifty dollars, and fifty dollars is fifty dollars!"

The pilot was a shrewd businessman, and he had noticed how much Grandma liked to talk. So he said, "Okay, I'll give you a special deal. I'll take you both up for a ride. If you can both stay quiet for the entire ride and not say one word, I won't charge you. But if you say one word, it's fifty dollars!"

Grandpa was delighted, and Grandma grudgingly agreed, so up they went.

The pilot performed all kinds of twists and turns, rolls and dives, but not a word was heard. He even did a nosedive, pulling up just above the ground, but still he didn't hear a word. Eventually he landed the plane and turned to Grandpa, who looked rather red in the face.

"Fair enough: I did my utmost to get you to yell out, but you didn't," said the pilot.

Grandpa replied, "Well, I almost said something when Grandma fell out, but fifty dollars is fifty dollars!"

Grandpa's Presents

Everyone knows that grandpas are impossible to buy for. But they are equally notorious for buying presents (especially for grandchildren) that are unsuitable, if not actually dangerous! You may therefore find your family keeping you under lock and key when birthdays or Christmas approach. Grandpas' presents are often the subject of disapproval and anxiety among parents, but grandchildren usually think they are fantastic!

Grandpa: Presents to Avoid

Although the following are all fun and will prove to be hugely popular with the children, you would be better off resisting them if you don't want to alienate the parents forever. Here, then, is Grandpa's "banned" list:

* **Water guns:** Under strict supervision in the backyard (never indoors), preferably shooting at an inanimate target, water guns can be quite safe. Unfortunately, when adult eyes are momentarily distracted, the poor cat is attacked or the pistol is filled with ink and squirted on the best carpet. Guaranteed to lead to arguments within the first twenty-four hours!

* **Stink bombs and other practical jokes:** Whoopee cushions are amusing, provided you're not holding a glass of red wine at the time. Stink bombs are even more

nauseating than anyone remembers, and the pungent smell lasts forever. Giving these as gifts will likely get the grandchild permanently excluded from any school he or she attends.

* **Musical instruments such as trumpets and drums:** Gifts that make a noise often generate great pleasure for the grandchild, who will parade around the house with gusto wearing a huge grin of pride. But parents' patience will wear thin quickly as listening to the television becomes impossible and concentration on this year's tax return is broken.

* **Darts:** Even though you've mounted the dartboard on an enormous backdrop, it's quite extraordinary how the darts will continuously miss both the board and what's behind it. Giving these as a gift is guaranteed to earn at least one member of the family a trip to the emergency room within a week.

* **Pets:** There are some fascinating animals available for sale these days. Whether the choice is as calming as a tropical fish, as scary as a snake, or as noisy as a parrot, one thing is for sure: It's the parents who will end up being the ones doing the feeding, the exercise, and the cleaning up.

* **Chemistry sets:** Fire department, police, or ambulance? You can confidently predict a visit from at least one of the emergency services as soon as the first experiment goes awry. The only question is which service it will be.

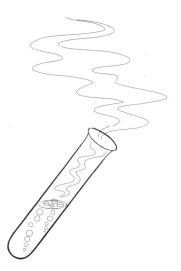

Avoid at All Costs

"Time is a dressmaker specializing in alterations."
FAITH BALDWIN, author

When you look in the mirror, you see an old man, but when you're with the grandkids, it's easy to forget. After all, at heart you feel as young as ever. Surely there's no harm in joining them for some tree climbing?

Yes, grandpas are notorious for being their own worst enemies: They're always up for a laugh and ready to be the life and soul of the party. However, the harsh reality is that, as a grandpa, you have to take care of yourself.

Here are some of the pitfalls faced by the grandfather species.

Tarzan Swinging

The day is bright, the car is packed, and you're off for a picnic in the hills. You come across a ravine. A long rope has been tied from the treetops, and an old tire beckons seductively at its end.

Your imagination beats in time with your racing heart. You'll show your grandchild a trick or two. You'll be Tarzan, swinging through the jungle.

When you wake up in the hospital bed, your three broken ribs swathed in bandages, you will realize that your vanity has exceeded your common sense.

The School Field Day

The school field day is the next high-risk temptation. It is so easy to be corralled, shamed, or bullied into the three-legged race or the sack race. Be on your guard! These medieval tortures have been proven by doctors to cause more muscle strains and torn ligaments than falling off skis in the Olympic downhill race.

Plan ahead. Have some excuses ready. Claim to be a professional who's not allowed to compete in an amateur race. Or join the volunteer paramedics so that you can justify standing at the finish line to watch some other poor guy pull his back out.

Things You Shouldn't Consume

✳ **Cups of coffee or tea before a long car trip.** The size of a grandpa's bladder has been proven to diminish in direct proportion to the number of cups of coffee consumed and in inverse proportion to the distance to the next rest stop.

✳ **Baked beans prior to going to the movies.** You can always blame the smell on the grandchild, of course, but no one wants to listen to an unseemly "You did it!" "No, you did it!" argument when they're trying to watch a tear-jerking love story.

* **Peanuts.** Beware the next time you are offered these innocent-looking snacks before dinner. They will penetrate your dentures, wriggling into the cavities only to emerge again during the meal so that you cough the mouthful of roast chicken into the middle of the table. You'll find you don't get invited back for a while.

Planning Ahead

While the common image of a grandfather is of an old man with a white beard, many men actually become grandfathers in their forties. So you might have several decades before you face retirement, but there's no doubt about it, becoming a grandpa makes you think more about what the future holds.

Keeping Busy in Retirement

Whether you're excited by the prospect of retirement or dreading it, it's always a good idea to plan ahead, and you'll soon realize it can be a golden opportunity to do the things you've always wanted to do. You can also use your extra time to make a difference in your local community in numerous different ways. How about some of the following ideas for inspiration?

Become a volunteer

Volunteer work offers the chance to interact with people of different ages. It's also a great way to use your skills and experience to help others and at the same time learn something new. Approach your favorite charity, as it will surely welcome your contribution.

Learn for fun

Learning can be fun, and it's a great way to relax and social-ize. It doesn't have to be formal, and you don't have to take any exams at the end unless you want to. Many adult edu-cation courses are inexpensive or even free. Try something you've never done before, from car mechanics to photography to learning Swahili! In addition to evening classes, there are many online courses available if you prefer to learn at your own pace at home. Or why not give yourself the challenge of simply learning a new skill, such as cooking the Sunday roast or tackling a plumbing job yourself?

Research your local history

Are you interested in history? Retirement is a great time to dis-cover more about the history of your family, community, or house. The local library is a good place to start (see opposite). Your grandchild might even be interested in helping you with the research, so why not ask?

Research local leisure activities

Find out about leisure activities for older people in your area on the Internet or at your local library or community center. These may include cultural events, sports events, and other organized social activities. They are a great way to make new friends in your vicinity.

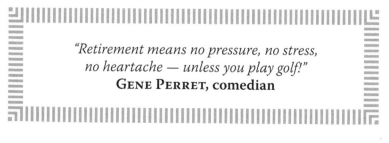

"Retirement means no pressure, no stress, no heartache — unless you play golf!"
GENE PERRET, comedian

Join the local library

You will enjoy many hours of pleasure from reading books found at your local library, but these days the library offers a whole lot more. Perhaps you would like to rent a DVD or video, or use the Internet free of charge, or get help with literacy skills. You'll find all of these services and more if you ask.

Keep fit and healthy

Making sure that you exercise regularly and keep an eye on what you eat is of real importance as you get older, both to improve your current physical and mental health and to protect your quality of life for the future.

Keeping mobile and active is the goal. Explore your local community center or gym to see if they offer activities such as swimming, tennis, squash, or aerobics classes.

Information on local and national sports events is also available. If you really don't want to be a participator, be a supporter of your local sports team.

Healthful eating can also help you control your weight: You will look trim and feel more fit. There's a lot you can do to introduce healthier foods into your diet without giving up some of your favorites. Speak to your doctor for advice and support if you don't know where to start.

Visit your local museums and art galleries

Want a day out that is fun and educational at the same time? You could try visiting a museum or art gallery. All over the country there are hundreds of exhibitions covering a wide variety of topics from local history to modern art. Why not take your grandchild with you?

Become a geek

The wonders of the Internet await you! Users over the age of fifty are set to dominate online shopping. To make the most of the Internet, you'll need basic computer skills. If you don't have those already, there are courses that can help you get started.

Explore your patch of the earth

You can take up fishing or enjoy a canoe trip down a local stream. Alternatively, you can find many green and pleasant open spaces in your local countryside where you can have a picnic, play outdoor games, go for a hike, or watch for wildlife. If you rarely leave the comfort of your town or city, then head for the great outdoors and embark on some adventures. And if you're really the outdoors type, you can join a local hiking or nature club.

Don't forget the gray matter

Keep your intellect active as well. Reading, completing crosswords, or playing chess all help keep the gray matter in good form. This is especially important as you get older. Remember the maxim "Use it or lose it!"

Money Matters

Planning for one's future financial security makes sense. There is a lot of advice available for the prudent grandpa or his family to make retirement more financially secure. Even if you don't have much money to spare, financial planning is really worth considering if there are some simple ways to economize and make your money work harder for you. There is no substitute for personalized independent financial advice, but the following are the kinds of areas you should be thinking about.

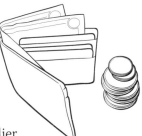

✳ Invest in a retirement plan. The earlier you start, the richer and more secure you will be in old age. However, it's never too late to invest in your future — or the future of your grandchild.

✳ Claim all the available benefits and tax reliefs to which you are entitled.

✳ Plan for the special needs you will face as you get older. For example, set aside money for extra winter fuel bills, or save for the extra help you might need if you become disabled or need personal care.

✳ Write a will and prepare for your dependents' financial security after you have gone.

"The challenge of retirement is how to spend time without spending money."
ANONYMOUS

Be sure to look for:

The GRANDMAS' Book

FOR THE GRANDMA WHO'S

Best AT Everything

Also available in this bestselling series: